A Funny Thing

Happened on the Way to the Thing

WHITE HOUSE

A Funny Thing

Happened on the Way to the

Thing

WHITE HOUSE

Foolhardiness, Folly, and Fraud
in Presidential Elections,
from Andrew Jackson
to George W. Bush

DAVID E. JOHNSON &
JOHNNY R. JOHNSON

TAYLOR TRADE PUBLISHING
Lanham • New York • Dallas • Boulder • Toronto • Oxford

Chapter 8 reprinted courtesy of Historical Times, Inc., publishers of *American History Illustrated.*

Copyright © 1983 by David E. Johnson and Johnny R. Johnson
First Taylor Trade Publishing edition 2004
Originally published in 1983 by Beaufort Books, Inc. Reprinted by permission.

Published by Taylor Trade Publishing
An imprint of The Rowman & Littlefield Publishing Group, Inc.
4501 Forbes Boulevard, Suite 200
Lanham, Maryland 20706

Distributed by National Book Network

Library of Congress Cataloging-in-Publication Data

The Beaufort Books edition of this book was previously catalogued by the Library of
Congress as follows:

Johnson, David E.
  A funny thing happened on the way to the White House.
  Bibliography: p.
    1. Presidents—United States—Anecdotes, facetiae, satire, etc. 1. Johnson,
  Johnny Ray. II. Title.
  E176.1.J63 1983 973'.09'92   83-7085

ISBN 1-58979-150-9 (pbk. : alk.paper)

♾™ The paper used in this publication meets the minimum requirements of
American National Standard for Information Sciences—Permanence of
Paper for Printed Library Materials, ANSI/NISO Z39.48–1992.
Manufactured in the United States of America.

Does [the art of politics] appear to be unqualifiedly ratty, raffish, sordid, obscene, and low down, and its salient virtuosi a gang of unmitigated scoundrels? Then let us not forget its high capacity to soothe and tickle the midriff, its incomparable services as a maker of entertainment.

— H. L. MENCKEN

Contents

Presidential Politics

We do not believe that the American people will knowingly elect to the presidency a coarse debauchee who would bring his harlots with him to Washington and hire lodgings for them convenient to the White House.

—*New York Sun* description of Grover Cleveland

American presidential politics has many notable traditions, but probably none is so time-honored or ubiquitous as the slinging of mud, and all of our presidents—from the most revered to the least regarded—have been on the receiving end.

Andrew Jackson's wife, for instance, was charged with being a bigamist. Thomas Jefferson's election, it was said, would set the "seal of death on our holy religion," and "prostitutes . . . will preside in the sanctuaries now devoted to the worship of the Most High." Abraham Lincoln, considered by many historians to be our greatest president, was attacked as "a low-bred, obscene clown," a "dishonest baboon," and "another Benedict Arnold." Even George Washington, whose superb leadership, integrity, and good judgment have secured his place of honor in our history, was called a tyrant, a dictator, and an imposter. One political cartoon even referred to him as an ass. Washington had no intention of setting a precedent when he declined a third term. He simply refused to take any more abuse.

It may be true, as Confucius said, that he who slings mud loses ground, but American political campaigners obviously don't believe it. In every presidential election, we have what the Englishman Sir James Bryce in the 1880s called "the spectacle of half the honest men supporting for the headship of the nation a person whom the other half declare to be a knave."

American politicians have also used humor as a weapon. At a 1963 press conference, a reporter told John F. Kennedy that the Republican National Committee had "adopted a resolution saying you were pretty much of a failure. . . . How do you feel about that?" Kennedy's reply completely destroyed the resolution's effectiveness. "I assume it passed unanimously," he said.

Even William Jennings Bryan, the evangelical, deadly serious Democratic candidate of 1896, 1900, and 1908, got into the act. On one occasion, when asked to address a crowd of farmers from the only available elevated stage, a manure spreader, he joked, "This is the first time I have ever spoken from a Republican platform."

And Republican-Progressive candidate Theodore Roosevelt in 1912, when accused of stealing Democratic Party platform planks, admitted it was "quite true. I have taken every one of them," he said, "except those suited for inmates of lunatic asylums."

Presidential candidates, however, must use wit carefully, for there is a thin line between being quick on one's feet and being considered a buffoon. In the 1952 campaign, Democrat Adlai Stevenson's quips were turned against him by what he called "the Republican law of gravity." Lincoln, whose humor is now part of our national heritage, was roundly condemned for telling funny stories against the tragic backdrop of the Civil War.

In some cases, candidates remained silent, perhaps believing the theory that it is better to keep one's mouth shut and be thought a fool than to open it and remove all doubt. For example, in 1868 it was said of

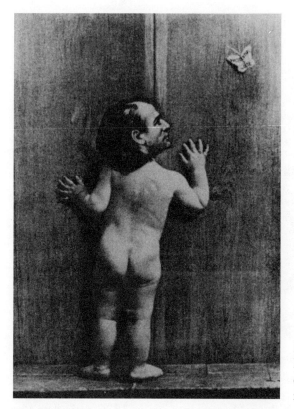

Little Billy Bryan Chasing Butterflies—an 1896 attack on the youthful Bryan that first appeared in *Judge*.

General U. S. Grant that he "refused to express his views, concealing the fact that he had none." No less a figure than John Adams had earlier disclosed similar uncharitable thoughts when he observed, "Washington got the reputation of being a great man because he kept his mouth shut." Of course, Calvin Coolidge was so noted for never saying *anything* that when humorist Dorothy Parker heard he had died, she quipped, "How can they tell?"

The Whig party, which was one of the two major parties from about 1832 until about 1856, specialized in keeping its candidates quiet during the campaign, leaving the hell-raising to others. Whig candidates, except for Henry Clay, were carefully selected generals whose views were unknown or nonexistent. An opponent remarked that "availability was the only ability" required of the Whig candidates. The

Lincoln as a monkey (Courtesy the Lilly Library, Indiana University, Bloomington).

strategy of General William Henry Harrison in 1836, articulated by his campaign manager, was typical: "Let no committee, no convention, no town meeting extract from him a single word about what he thinks now or what he will do hereafter."

Campaign rhetoric has improved little, if at all, since the earliest presidential elections, but political strategies and methods have changed radically through the years. One welcome change is that the vice president, presiding over the Senate, no longer feels the need to take loaded pistols to work with him as Martin Van Buren did. No president since John Tyler has issued guns to the White House staff to defend him against his enemies, although the thought may have occurred to Richard Nixon in 1973 and 1974. Indeed, we have come a long way from the relatively uncomplicated times when President Washington could say of his ambassador to France: "We haven't heard from Benjamin Franklin in Paris this year. We should write him a letter."

"I CANNOT TELL THE TRUTH."

President Grant as a drunkard and a liar.

From Washington's day to Lincoln's, no presidential candidate campaigned openly for himself. Such antics were considered too undignified for the aspirant to such a noble office. Lincoln even refused to vote for himself, but finally consented to clip his own name off the ballot and vote for the rest of his party's ticket.

Stephen A. Douglas, Lincoln's Democratic opponent in 1860, was the first candidate to stump openly, and his campaigning was offensive to most voters. The *Jonesboro* (Illinois) *Gazette* said at the time, "Douglas is going about peddling his opinions as a tin man peddles his ware. The only excuse for him is that as he is a small man, he has a right to be engaged in small business; and small business it is for a candidate for the Presidency to be strolling around the country begging for votes like a town constable."

Douglas, of course, was aware of the precedent he was setting and tried to maintain the fiction that his trips were nonpolitical (a practice

An 1848 cartoon of Zachary Taylor as the Whig candidate (typically with no qualifications) and a general who killed many soldiers.

that continues today). One of those trips was a visit paid to his mother in Clifton Springs, New York. On this occasion a New Hampshire paper gibed that to get from Illinois to New York, he "naturally came to New Haven, Guilford, and Hartford on his way, and . . . was 'betrayed' into a speech." Again "at Worcester some Judas 'betrayed' him into a speech. At Boston, 'betrayed' again."

In the modern presidential campaign, candidates travel thousands of miles and deliver hundreds of speeches. Jet planes and television have made a great difference, but the flowery prose, the pratfalls, the outrageous gibes, and the bilge go on and on.

Despite its "warts and all," to use Nixon's Watergate line, the presidential campaign is a uniquely American institution that has served us well. When a firm hand was essential to guide the new nation in 1788, Washington was available. Jefferson boldly doubled our country's size

WHO IS NEXT?

RIGHT

An 1892 lampooning of the possible Republican candidates to face Cleveland (looking on from the window). The current sitter on the pot is the incumbent president, Benjamin Harrison.

with the Louisiana Purchase, in spite of criticism from his short-sighted opponents who claimed, "The United States are now doomed to pay a large sum for a vast wilderness world which will . . . prove worse than useless to us. . . . Every man, woman, and child is saddled with a debt of $4.36." When most of the conventional wisdom (including that of young Congressman Abraham Lincoln) opposed the annexation of Texas and one major party candidate campaigned against it, James K. Polk appeared as the first dark-horse candidate and won with the determination to annex not only Texas but California and the Pacific Northwest as well. At the country's most dangerous period since Valley Forge, Lincoln emerged to guide the country through the Civil War. Woodrow Wilson led us through World War I, and we had Franklin D. Roosevelt to attack the Great Depression and command the mightiest military force in history in World War II.

No matter who has been elected to the White House, every four years we've been treated to an entertaining and exciting show. So let's

take a fond look backward at a number of the most interesting and colorful of our presidential elections—from the first popular contest in 1828
to the television extravaganzas of today.

Look askance, if you wish, at the rhetoric, invective, and humor
slung by each side at the other, but remember that all's fair in love and
politics, and a little slander or a few well-placed potshots are as American
as apple pie. Consider that John Calvin himself said that politics is the
noblest profession, and pay no attention to the ever-present naysayers
who don't like any candidate. A lot can be said in defense of a spirited
and hard-fought campaign. The whole performance is, after all, designed
to select the best individual for the job. We may not agree on every qualification, but certainly all our presidents have passed the muster of
Republican statesman Chester Congdon, who said in 1916 on another
subject, "Damn it gentlemen, what I want for this job is a man the dogs
won't urinate on."

Old Hickory

The election of 1828 was the first in which electors were popularly chosen. In the words of the candidates' detractors, it was a race between a "pimp" and a "convicted adulterer." The candidates' real names were John Quincy Adams and Andrew Jackson, and the election was almost a replay of the 1824 contest in which Adams was elected over Jackson even though Old Hickory had more electoral votes. Indeed, many said the 1828 campaign lasted four years, beginning immediately after Adams was inaugurated and had appointed his cabinet.

The House of Representatives decided the 1824 election because no candidate had an electoral vote majority. The Speaker of the House, Henry Clay, had finished fourth in the election and was influential in electing Adams. General Jackson had mercilessly beaten and even killed men for lesser offenses, but he was remarkably calm this time, taking his defeat with gentlemanly good grace—at first.

Adams had all the qualifications for the presidency, unless political astuteness is one of them. He demonstrated this flaw in his makeup immediately by determining, upon taking office, that the man best qualified to be secretary of state was Henry Clay. After all, Clay had been sufficiently qualified to prefer Adams to Jackson. The Jacksonians howled their indignation. They set up a cry of "corrupt bargain" that was to make Adams, like his father, a one-term president and was to dog Henry Clay throughout his lifelong struggle to be president. The legislature of Tennessee, Jackson's home state, passed a resolution of condemnation: "Mr. Adams desired the office of President; he went into the combination without it, and came out with it. Mr. Clay desired that of Secretary of State; he went into the combination without it, and came out with it." Could anything be plainer? Jackson himself charged that a "bargain and sale of the constitutional rights of the people" had been effected. Of Clay's appointment, Old Hickory wrote, "So you see the Judas of the West has closed the contract and will receive the thirty pieces of silver. His end will be the same. Was there ever witnessed such a barefaced corruption?"

King Andrew the First—Jackson trampling on the constitution.

The hostilities recessed briefly in 1828 for the nominations of the candidates. Since the Federalist Party's death, around 1816, both major candidates had come from different wings of Jefferson's Democratic-Republican Party. The Jacksonians, calling themselves Democrats, nominated John C. Calhoun as Jackson's running mate. Adams's faction nominated Richard Rush for vice president. Rush previously had been appointed secretary of the treasury under President Monroe, a move condemned by the great American master of invective, Senator John Randolph of Virginia, as "the worst appointment since the Roman emperor Caligula appointed his horse Consul." (Rush got off relatively easily. Randolph once declared statesman Edward Livingston "utterly corrupt. Like rotten mackerel by moonlight, he shines and stinks.")

There was no such objection raised this time to Rush, at least not equal to the caliber of Randolph's, so the battle was joined between "John Quincy Adams, who can write, / And Andrew Jackson, who can fight."

So went a ditty of the time, in a more or less valid assessment of the two candidates. Jackson was not a man of letters, as Adams observed when he referred to him as a "barbarian and savage who can scarcely spell his own name." The general believed that the earth was flat, spelled Europe "Urop," and was said to have read only one book all the way through in his life—*The Vicar of Wakefield*, oddly enough. Adams, on the other hand, was an intellectual and a very able man, but—like his father before him—he seemed to have unconcealed contempt for the voters, a flaw that is usually fatal in elected officials. For example, he once told the Congress not to give the rest of the world the impression "that we are palsied by the will of our constituents." Until he read that speech, Jackson said, he thought Adams had "a tolerable share of common sense."

The campaign was exceedingly dirty, with both sides reaching new depths of scurrility. The voters were constantly reminded of Adams's "corrupt bargain" and his "infamous Coalition" with Clay. Adams was a "usurper" of the presidency, whose chess set and billiard table, purchased with his own money, became "gaming tables and gambling furniture." Jackson was denounced as a liar, a thief, a drunkard, a bigamist, an adulterer, a gambler, a cockfighter, a Negro trader, and a murderer. The Dutch voters in Pennsylvania and New York were told by the Jacksonians, in words so solemn as to seem like documented facts, that the friends of

Adams's Coalition "have heretofore spoken of the Dutch, calling them the black Dutch, the stupid Dutch, the ignorant Dutch, and other names equally decorous and civil." The general, on the other hand, "revered" the Dutch for their patriotism and countless other virtues. Jackson, in the eyes of the opposition, was an ignorant, cruel, bloodthirsty man, who was "quite insane." A political handbook said: "You know that he is no jurist, no statesman, no politician; that he is destitute of historical, political, or statistical knowledge; that he is unacquainted with the orthography, concord, and government of his language; you know that he is a man of no labor, no patience, no investigation; in short that his whole recommendation is animal fierceness and organic energy. He is wholly unqualified by education, habit, and temper for the station of President."

In a less serious vein, a Democratic newspaper published puns and jokes about the opposition:

"Hurrah for Jackson," said one man.

"Hurrah for the Devil," replied a Jackson-hater.

"Very well," retorted the first man. "You stick to your candidate, and I'll stick to mine."

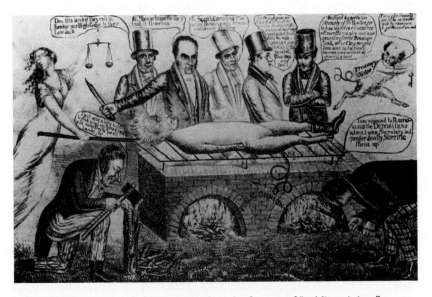

Jackson as a hog being barbecued on the furnace of "public opinion."

Many stories were told to illustrate Adams's disdain for common-
ers. One likened the Adams supporters among the plain people to the
Frenchman who bragged that King Louis had spoken to him:

"What did the king say to you?" asked an impressed friend.

"He told me to get out of his way," was the reply.

Clay's name provided grist for the punsters. The puns were awful,
of course—and in this respect little has changed since 1828.

"Why is Adams on ticklish ground?"

"Because he stands on slippery Clay."

With these preliminaries and inanities taken care of, both sides got
down to serious business. The chief ammunition against Jackson was the
Coffin Hand Bill, a circular that purported to give "Some account of some
of the Bloody Deeds of GENERAL JACKSON." It gave the names of
six soldiers who had been tried and executed shortly after the battle
of New Orleans for crimes of robbery, arson, mutiny, and desertion. Their

Jackson as "Richard III: Methought
the souls of all that I had murder'd
came to my tent."

trials were perfectly legal, and they had been executed strictly according to law. But the handbill referred to them as "victims" of Old Hickory's callous cruelty. Under each name was the picture of a huge black coffin, and a description was given of the "murders" of the "innocent" men. Included was a poem entitled "Mournful Tragedy," which contained verses like:

Sure he will spare! Sure JACKSON yet
Will all reprieve but one—
O hark! those shrieks! that cry of death!
The deadly deed is done!

One Democrat lightheartedly challenged the Coffin Hand Bill: "Pshaw! Why don't you tell the whole truth? On the 8th of January, 1815, he murdered in the coldest blood 1,500 British soldiers for merely trying to get into New Orleans in search of booty and beauty." Another Jackson supporter was more outraged. The public could now discern, he said, the thorough corruption of the administration. Adams and Clay conceived this "despicable broadside to strip the honored laurel from [Jackson's] brow."

Prostitution and debauchery also played a central role in the campaign. The Jacksonians circulated the story that Adams introduced a young American chambermaid to Czar Alexander when Adams was ambassador to Russia. The story was perfectly true, according to Adams, and the girl was introduced to the czar at the czar's request and in the presence of his wife. The czar was curious, said Adams, since the chambermaid had written a letter, intercepted by Russian authorities, recounting the czar's reputed love affairs. It was all in good humor, according to Adams, and the letter afforded the Russian royal couple "some amusement." Based on the incident, Jackson's supporters charged that Adams was "a practicing pimp," a procurer of American girls for the czar. The Democrats mocked Adams as "The Pimp of the Coalition" and noted that his activities as a procurer explained his fabulous success as a diplomat.

On the other side, the *Cincinnati Gazette* reported, "General Jackson's mother was a *COMMON PROSTITUTE* brought to this country by the British soldiers! She afterwards married a *MULATTO MAN*, with whom she had several children, of which General *JACKSON IS*

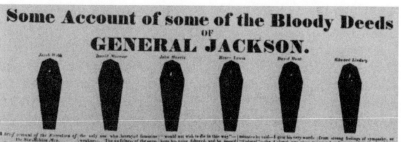

The Coffin Hand Bill, picturing Jackson as a murderer.

ONE!" One issue revealed that Jackson's "older brother was sold as a slave in Carolina."

The slander that most enraged Jackson was the attack on his wife, Rachel Donelson. Andrew and Rachel had married under the mistaken impression that she was legally divorced from her first husband. The couple was innocent of intentional wrongdoing, and when the awful truth was discovered shortly afterward, they dissolved the marriage. They repeated their vows four months later, after the divorce was obtained.

For the 1828 campaign the *Cincinnati Gazette* dredged up this story and charged that Jackson had prevailed upon Rachel to desert her husband and "live with him in the character of a wife." Anyone else would have been jailed for "open and notorious lewdness," but not Old Hickory. His reward was a presidential nomination. "Ought a convicted adulteress and her paramour husband to be placed in the highest offices of this free and Christian land?" asked the *Gazette*. "If General Jackson should be elected President," declared another Adams supporter, "what effect, think you, fellow-citizens, will it have upon the American youth?"

All of these charges were calculated to provoke Jackson into such a fit of rage that he would kill someone (presumably not Adams). "How hard it is to keep the cowhide from the villains," the general fumed, and he threatened to challenge Clay to a duel. Fortunately for Jackson—and doubtless also for Clay—he was talked out of this notion and managed more or less to contain himself.

"Clay is managing Adams' campaign," said a Jacksonian, "not like a statesman of the cabinet, but like a shyster, pettifogging in a bastard suit before a country squire." Jackson, however, held Adams responsible. "He is certainly the basest, meanest scoundrel that ever disgraced the image of his God. Nothing is too mean or low for him to condescend to to secretly carry his cowardly and base purposes of slander into effect. Even the aged and virtuous female is not free from his secret combinations of base slander." In one of her last letters, Rachel Jackson gave her views: "The enemys of the Genl have dipt their arrows in wormwood and gall and sped them at me . . . thaey have Disquieted one that they had no rite to do." She added that she would rather be "a doorkeeper in the house of God than to live in that palace at Washington."

"*Jackson is to be President, and you will be HANGED.*"

Jackson performing a hanging.

On election day both sides put on a massive get-out-the-vote drive, which would compare favorably with those of today. In New York, where Adams's fortunes had dramatically improved with the death of his archenemy, Governor De Witt Clinton (an event referred to by Clay as a "fortuitous demise"), Jackson's ally Martin Van Buren urged on his followers. He reminded them not to "forget to bet all you can." An Ohioan complained to Clay that if Tennessee "disgorges one thousand voters upon us, we are gone." He explained that his side would have only "two or three thousand illegal ones of our own." The Jacksonians were so certain of attempts at fraud that they used poll watchers, a practice that was new then but is common now.

The result was a resounding victory for Jackson, who received 178 electoral votes to 83 for Adams. The opposition did not have even the thread of hope that they were to have four years later, when Jackson won reelection by demolishing Clay. That hope was the "one comfort left: God has promised that the days of the wicked shall be short; the wicked [Jackson] is old and feeble, and he may die before [the Electoral College can meet]. It is the duty of every good Christian to pray for our Maker to have pity on us."

Jackson's victory was marred by the death of his beloved Rachel only a few weeks after the 1828 election. He blamed his enemies for her death, and at her funeral he swore: "In the presence of this dear saint I can and do forgive all my enemies. But those vile wretches who have slandered her must look to God for mercy."

Andrew Jackson was a new kind of president. Under him the country was not "ruined past redemption," as his enemies feared—but its course was thoroughly altered. He was the first popularly elected president (before him the electors were chosen largely by the legislatures and an aristocratic minority), and he acted for all the people. He left office in 1837 with, he said, but two regrets. He was sorry he didn't "shoot Henry Clay and hang John C. Calhoun." As one historian has said of Jackson, "More than one such president a century would be hard to take. Yet he was a giant in his influence on our system . . . and second only to Washington in terms of influence on the Presidency." In a national crisis Americans might say, as men of goodwill did in 1861, "O for one hour of Andrew Jackson!"

Tippecanoe and Tyler Too

The first truly modern campaign was probably that of 1840, called by one historian the "jolliest and most idiotic in our history." An incumbent president was attacked for taking baths, his opponent was chosen because he had no views—and a committee was formed to see that he didn't develop any—and there was a vice presidential candidate whose main qualification seemed to be that he had once killed a man. The losing party was "sung down, lied down, and drunk down." One newspaper hoped after the election that the "buffoonery of 1840" would never again be repeated but would "stand solitary and alone, on the page of history, a damning stain on the brow of Federalism."

The incumbent president running for reelection was the Democrat Martin Van Buren, who had been handpicked by Andrew Jackson to be his successor four years earlier. Van Buren was from Kinderhook, New York, and called himself Old Kinderhook, the initials of which gave birth to the slang expression O.K. The *New York Morning Herald* unkindly suggested that the letters stood for Jackson's "illiterate method" of saying "Ole Kurrek (all correct)." The Democrats used O.K. affectionately, but the Whigs turned it around to indicate what they intended to make Van Buren in November: "K.O. for Kicked Out."

The times were wild, and invective flowed freely. William Seward, later to be Lincoln's secretary of state and the prime mover in the purchase of Alaska, castigated Van Buren as "a crawling reptile, whose only claim was that he had inveigled the confidence of a credulous, blind, dotard, old man [Jackson]." Another critic said, "The searching look of his keen eyes showed that he believed . . . that Language was given to conceal thought." History has judged Van Buren an able president who became vulnerable to political attack because of hard times caused by the Panic of 1837. It's unfortunate that he is remembered mainly for being the first president born under our constitution, for coining a new slang expression, and for bathing regularly.

The Whigs nominated General William Henry Harrison, whose principal virtues were that he had no known views and was a military hero. (A "hero of forty defeats," his enemies said.) He was also the titular head of the party, having lost to Van Buren in the previous election of 1836. By 1840 he was sixty-eight years old—the oldest candidate ever nominated for the presidency by a major party until Ronald Reagan in 1980.

"A Hard Row to Hoe!"—Jackson leading Van Buren back to the White House, which was "O.K."

A hostile view of Van Buren.

Harrison was the commanding general at the battle of Tippecanoe in 1811. He defeated the Indian chief Tecumseh, who was defending the Indians' hunting grounds against encroachment by the white man. Harrison became known as Old Tippecanoe and was presidential timber from that point on. (In those days all generals were called old something or other, like today's bourbon whiskeys. Andrew Jackson was known as Old Hickory; Zachary Taylor, Old Rough and Ready; and Winfield Scott, Old Fuss and Feathers.)

The Whigs chose John Tyler, a Democrat, as Harrison's running mate. The battle cry of 1840 thus became "Tippecanoe and Tyler too." A Whig who cared little for Tyler said of the addition to the ticket, "There was rhyme but no reason in it."

Henry Clay, who coveted the Whig nomination and had fully expected to get it, was furious at the selection of Harrison. "My friends are not worth the powder and shot it would take to kill them!" he exclaimed. "If there were two Henry Clays, one of them would make

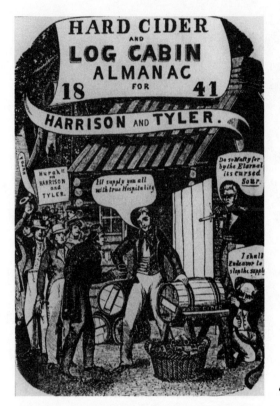

"Hurrah for Old Tippecanoe."

the other President of the United States. . . . I am the most unfortunate man in the history of parties: always run by my friends when sure to be defeated, and now betrayed for a nomination when I, or any one, would be sure of an election." The *New Orleans Bee* agreed: "Just think of a man such as Mr. Clay . . . without whom the Whig party would not this day exist, cast aside for a driveller."

As for the Democrats, their incumbent vice president, Richard Mentor Johnson, was said actually to have killed Tecumseh. It also was said that he "openly and shamefully lives in adultery with a buxom young Negro." This and other rumors lost him the support of Jackson, who predicted, "If Col Johnson is the nominee it will loose the democracy [that is, the Democratic party] thousand of votes." The convention therefore decided not to renominate Johnson—indeed it nominated no one for the vice presidency—but he was allowed to run on his own. This he did, with the slogan "Rumpsey-dumpsey, rumpsey-dumpsey. Colonel Johnson killed Tecumseh."

This rhythmic couplet, a holdover from the 1836 election, was a portent of things to come. The *Baltimore Republican* set the tone of the campaign when it published the reaction of a disgruntled Clay disciple to Harrison's nomination: "Get rid of . . . [Harrison]! and pray tell . . . how are we to do it?" The writer of the article supplied the answer: "Give him a barrel of hard cider, and settle a pension of two thousand a year on him, and my word for it, he will sit the remainder of his days in a log cabin by the side of a 'seacoal' fire and study moral philosophy."

The Democrats republished this piece of foolishness to taunt the Whigs, but the latter seized on it as an opportunity sent from heaven. They made Harrison the "log cabin and hard cider candidate" and also made the Democrats look like the party of the rich. "General Harrison is sneered at by the Eastern office-holders' pimps, as the 'Log-Cabin Candidate,'" declared one Whig newspaper. "Never mind! [Log-cabin dwellers] have a way of taking care of themselves, when insulted, which has sometimes surprised folks." Another said, "Log-Cabin Candidate is the term of reproach . . . [of] pampered office-holders . . . [who] sneer at the idea of making a *poor man* President of the United States." Actually, Harrison was far from poor—he lived in a mansion on the Ohio River—but this made no difference to anybody.

After that the Whigs did not need to debate the issues or to try to hide the fact that their candidate had no views. They simply used the slogans about log cabins and hard cider and made up countless songs to drown out anyone who tried to talk sense. As the Whig managers correctly observed, "Passion and prejudice, properly aroused and directed, will do about as well as principle and reason in a party contest." Modern campaign techniques, as some cynics would say, thus were first used in the election of 1840.

What about the issue of the independent treasury? The Whigs replied:

Jackson and Van Buren as "Uncle Sam's Pet Pups," being trapped by General Harrison.

Hush-a-bye-baby;
Daddy's a Whig.
When he comes home
Hard cider he'll swig.

Was Harrison planning to reestablish the national bank?

Let Van from his coolers of silver drink wine
And lounge on his cushioned settee,
Our man on a buckeye bench can recline,
Content with hard cider is he.

There were enough Whig rhymes and songs to fill a book. Horace Greeley collected the most popular ones and published them in the *Log Cabin Song Book*, which became the psalmbook of the campaign.

The Whigs held mass meetings, measuring attendance by the acre: "Six acres of men heard General Harrison." They organized parades with

"It is the ball a-rolling on for Tippecanoe and Tyler too."

floats exhibiting log cabins and barrels of hard cider. Campaign souvenirs and merchandise, featuring such items as Tippecanoe Shaving Soap, Log Cabin Emollient, Harrison and Tyler neckties, and pocket brandy and whiskey bottles in the shape of log cabins, were sold everywhere. The Old Cabin Whiskey in these unique containers was supplied by the E. C. Booz Distillery, which contributed to the language another word, booze, for liquor. The Whigs also built large, heavy, paper balls with political slogans written on them, which they pulled through the crowds at campaign stops. From these shenanigans evolved our expressions "Keep the ball rolling" and "On the ball."

With all their electioneering gimmicks, the Whigs still had time for Van Buren. He was called Sweet Sandy Whiskers and was ridiculed as a fop "laced up in corsets, such as women in town wear, and, if possible, tighter than the best of them." Davy Crockett and Congressman Charles Ogle launched the most vicious attacks, with the latter delivering a three-day speech in the House on "The Regal Splendor of the President's Palace." According to Ogle, the White House "palace" grounds had rare plants and shrubs, and "clever sized hills" constructed in pairs "to resemble . . . an Amazon's bosom, with a miniature knoll or hillock on its apex, to denote the nipple." The inside of the White House contained "silk tassels, galloon, gimp and satin medallion to beautify and adorn the Blue Elliptical Saloon." The climax came when Ogle revealed that a bathtub had been installed in the White House and that Van Buren was "the first President [to insist upon] the pleasures of the warm or tepid bath [as] proper accompaniments of a palace life."

Ogle's speech was made up of lies, of course (except, one would hope, the part about Van Buren's taking baths), but this did not deter the Whigs from using it and taunting the Democrats with it throughout the campaign. The speech was serialized on the front pages of leading newspapers, and Whig speakers traveled with it in their saddlebags. "Mr. Van Buren was in such a rage at reading Mr. Ogle's speech," a Louisville paper said, "that he actually burst his corset."

To counter the Democratic charges that he was "an imbecile on leading strings," Harrison decided to make speeches himself, thereby becoming the first presidential candidate to stump. It was hardly out-and-out stumping, as Douglas did in 1860, or as we know it today. He "was not actually let loose," one Democrat asserted, "but the rope only a little lengthened, like that of a pet 'possum, to exercise his limbs."

He spoke chiefly on safe issues like monarchy in government, which he was foursquare against, and he urged citizens to effect reform "peacefully if you can," for otherwise "the tyrants of Europe" would rejoice. Occasionally his practice of speaking out of both sides of his mouth got him into trouble—or would have in a sane campaign. He wrote a northern congressman, for instance, that the suggestion that he favored slavery was a vile slander, and to a southerner he said that he had "done and suffered more to support Southern rights than any person north of Mason and Dixon's line." He urged each correspondent to keep the opinions he expressed confidential. At length a committee was formed to screen Harrison's correspondence and make sure that a "cuckoo did not fly out of his mouth."

An army of Whigs took to the hustings to praise Old Tippecanoe. One defender was a former representative, Sergeant S. Prentiss of Mississippi, who was proud to defend such causes as "the fair flower of womanhood" from the "pestilential effluvia" of the Democrats. On one occasion, a Van Buren supporter hissed as Prentiss delivered his usual vitriol. Prentiss stopped, pointed at his detractor, and announced,

"Rome was once saved by the hissing of a goose, but I doubt if this republic ever will be."

Harrison and Tyler won the election by a big electoral vote margin. An incredible 78 percent of eligible voters went to the polls, no doubt because of the lively campaign. But the defeated side claimed that the "vast increase in votes" was accomplished by "mercenaries—hired, bribed and purchased wretches which the corruption fund has secured for the Whig ticket."

After the weird campaign was over, and it was "O.K." for Van Buren to return to Kinderhook, one newspaper editor expressed the hope that "No more may the world see coons, cabins, and cider usurp the place of principles, nor doggerel verse elicit a shout, while argument, principle and reason are passed by with a derisive sneer." After every campaign such hopes are voiced.

As an epilogue to the "jolly" and "idiotic" election of 1840, Harrison was inaugurated on March 4, 1841, and died a month later—"the deed of a kind and overruling Providence," according to Jackson. The official cause of death was pneumonia, but some cynics said Harrison died of doctors. The medical men "blistered" and "cupped" him and administered opium, camphor, brandy, crude petroleum, and snake weed. Since the last two were Indian medicine remedies, Harrison may have been finished, as one historian said, by "Tecumseh's revenge." The redoubtable poet William Cullen Bryant, in one of his lesser-known efforts, regretted Harrison's death "only because he did not live long enough to prove his incapacity for the office of President."

Fifty-Four Forty or Fight

The Whigs were denied the fruits of their tumultuous 1840 campaign victory by the early death of President Harrison. Not only were both houses of Congress Democratic but also, thanks to the Whigs' determination to straddle the issues, the Democrat John Tyler, whom they had chosen as Harrison's running mate, was now president. President Tyler, or "His Accidency," as John Quincy Adams called him, proceeded to act more like a Jacksonian Democrat than a Whig, with the result that at the end of his term he was, in the words of the New York boss Thurlow Weed, "the poor, miserable, despised imbecile, who now goes from the Presidential chair, scorned of all parties."

The Whigs were determined to run more conventional candidates in the 1844 campaign. They nominated sixty-seven-year-old Henry Clay, who had lusted after the presidency all his adult life, giving him his third and apparently his last nomination. One of Clay's claims to fame was his statement, "I would rather be right than President," which writer Irving Stone labeled "the sourest grape since Aesop originated his fable."

For vice president the Whigs nominated Theodore Frelinghuysen, "a Christian gentleman," who was selected to balance Clay's "fluent profanity" and "known fondness for drinking and gambling."

The Democrats nominated James K. Polk—the first dark-horse candidate—for president and George M. Dallas for vice president. The party thus passed over "a man of ability like Van Buren" and in the words of the *National Intelligencer*, "let itself down" to Polk. "A more ridiculous, contemptible and forlorn candidate was never put forth by any party," said the *New York Herald*.

"Who the hell is Polk?" the Whigs gleefully shouted, making this their campaign cry. Clay had another view, though he kept it private. He had known Polk in Congress, and on the occasion of Polk's retirement as Speaker of the House in 1839, Clay had jeered from the galleries, "Go home, God damn you! Go home where you belong!" The story is told that Clay was relaxing at his home when his son rushed in and asked him to guess who had received the Democratic nomination. "Why, Matty [Van Buren], of course," said Clay. "No, guess again." "Cass?" "No." "Buchanan?" "No." Then Clay laughed, "Don't tell me they've been such fools as to take Calhoun or Johnson." His son again said no, and the exasperated Clay demanded, "Then who the devil is it?" When he

Clay and Polk as "Political Cockfighters."

heard the name "James K. Polk," he slowly poured himself a drink, sat down, and said, "Beat again, by God!"

The main issue of the campaign was the annexation of Texas, or to use the phrase of the times, the "reannexation" of Texas. Both Van Buren and Clay, the leaders of their respective parties, were against annexation, and in Van Buren's case it lost him his party's nomination. Before the convention Clay wrote that he considered annexation "as a measure compromising the national character, involving us certainly in a war with Mexico." As the campaign progressed, however, he saw that his stand was unpopular, and by the end of July he stated, "I have no hesitation in saying that, far from having any personal objection to the annexation of Texas, I should be glad to see it, without dishonor, without war."

His attitude angered the northern Whig leaders, who wanted the issue to be "Polk, slavery, and Texas," versus "Clay, Union, and liberty." One Whig declared that Clay "is rotten as a stagnant fish pond . . . and always has been. Confound him and all his compromises from first to last." Two days later, Clay, unnerved by the reaction, declared flatly, "I am decidedly opposed to the immediate annexation of Texas to the United States." He added that his statements "were not inconsistent," and that he would "write no further letters for publication on any public question." His flip-flops provided the Democratic press with a field day. Stealing the idea of verse from the Whigs of 1840, one editor wrote of Clay:

> He wires in and wires out,
> And leaves the people still in doubt,
> Whether the snake that made the track,
> Was going South, or coming back.

The Democrats shrewdly advocated not only the "reannexation of Texas" but also the "reoccupation of Oregon." The *re* was used to establish the claims that Oregon was ours by settlement and treaty, and that Texas was originally part of the Louisiana Purchase. In the case of Oregon, Polk campaigned for the entire territory up to latitude 54°40' north, giving rise to the Democratic campaign slogan "Fifty-Four Forty or Fight." (As president, he later settled for the forty-ninth parallel, but he got all of Mexico north of the Rio Grande River.)

The campaign was not nearly as lively as that of 1840, since the Whigs seemed to have lost some of their ardor. There was, however, enough vitriol to go around. Clay was called morally unfit for the presidency and said to be a duelist, a heavy drinker, and an inordinate gambler who was the inventor of the poker game. Polk was "an infidel from Tennessee" (the last part of which was true), a slaveholder who abused his slaves, a haughty tyrant, a pliant tool, and a petty scoundrel. "Clay spends his days at a gaming table and his nights in a brothel," one Democrat said. Another said Clay's standard should be "a pistol, a pack of cards, and a brandy bottle." The *New York American* said that someone had seen "Polk's slaves on their way to die in the sugar mills of Louisiana" with "JKP burned into their flesh." Another paper said that the annexation of Texas, favored by Polk, was "a step conceived by traitors and base conspirators against the Union."

Clay was castigated by one Democrat as "notorious for his fiendish and vindictive speech, for his disregard of the most important moral obligations, for his blasphemy, for his gambling propensities, and for his

Tyler as an ass, Polk as a goose, and Van Buren as a fox, auctioned off by Clay "for want of use."

frequent and bloodthirsty attempts upon the lives of his fellow-men." This Democratic propagandist went on to say that Clay had violated all of the Ten Commandments and gave examples—except for those, such as "Mr. Clay's debaucheries and midnight revelries in Washington," that were "too shocking, too disgusting to appear in public print."

The voters, it seemed, had little choice as far as religious morality was concerned, what with Clay's repeated "violations of the decalogue" on the one hand, and the "infidel" Polk on the other. It was pointed out that Polk came by his impiety honestly, as anyone could see from the epitaph of his grandfather Ezekiel Polk, which was clearly carved on "durable wood" and was standing above his grave. It was a twenty-line poem that Ezekiel had composed himself, containing such couplets as:

Polk up a tree, calculated to hearten Whigs and discourage Democrats.

To holy cheats was never willing
To give one solitary shilling;

and

First Fruits and tenths are odious things,
So are bishops, priests and kings.

Working the other side of the morality issue, Sam Houston, the hero of the Texas civil war with Mexico, said that Polk was "the victim of the use of water as a beverage."

On the lighter side, the Democrats used slogans and songs, as the Whigs had four years earlier. The Whigs were referred to as "coons," a favorite term of Andrew Jackson, and the Democrats called themselves "coon skinners of 1844." In answer to the Whig question "Who is Polk?" they replied, "The K in Col. Polk's name is understood to stand for 'Koonkiller.'" They set this rhyme to music and sang it in the streets:

Blow the trumpet, beat the drum
Run Clay coons, we come. We come.

Polk won the election by the narrow margin of 1,337,243 votes against Clay's 1,299,062. When New York's 36 electoral votes were still in doubt, Polk had 134 electoral votes to Clay's 105. Eventually Polk won New York, and the election, by 4,000 votes. Young Abraham Lincoln, at the time an ardent Whig, lamented that if an abolitionist third party had not been in the field, New York would have "voted with us. . . . Mr. Clay would now be President . . . and Texas not annexed." True enough, but if the ticket of Polk and Dallas had not prevailed, the second-largest city in Texas today might carry the name of Santa Anna, or even worse, Frelinghuysen.

Another future president who did not share Polk's enthusiasm for Texas, Oregon, and California was General Zachary Taylor, who succeeded Polk. Taylor and Polk made a "strangely contrasting pair" in March 1849, as they rode together down Pennsylvania Avenue for Taylor's

"This is the House that Polk Built"—indicating how frail Polk's support was for his schemes.

inauguration: Polk, the studious, "proud master of every detail of the Presidency," and Taylor, the rough, unsophisticated old soldier. The outgoing president must have winced at Taylor's casual remark that "California and Oregon are both too far away." The "people out there" should be allowed to "form an independent government of their own." At the end of the ceremony, Polk said to the new president, "I hope, sir, the country will be prosperous under your administration," but in his diary he wrote that Taylor "was exceedingly ignorant of public affairs, and . . . of very ordinary capacity."

Who was James K. Polk? He was the president who fulfilled America's Manifest Destiny by expanding its borders across the continent from the Atlantic to the Pacific. "No man and no administration was ever more assailed, and none ever achieved more," said the *New York*

Sun upon Polk's death. It is ironic that, for all his accomplishments, Polk was vilified at the end of his term as "Polk the Mendacious" and "the little mole." Three months later he died of "chronic diarrhea."

Andrew Jackson's comment could be Polk's epitaph. The old general was overjoyed when Polk was elected and sent him the following message: "Who is j.k. polk will be no more asked by the coons—A.J." Who indeed was James K. Polk? He was the only strong president between Jackson and Lincoln and deserves to be ranked with the great ones. He knew what he wanted to do; it was more than almost any other president has ever done; he said he could do it in only one term; and he did it.

Honest Abe

" Mr. Lincoln is already beaten," said Horace Greeley in August 1864. "He cannot be elected. And we must have another ticket to save us from utter overthrow." The *New York World* said, "Honest old Abe has few honest men to defend his honesty." These were two of the more charitable views of Abraham Lincoln and his chances for reelection in the summer of 1864. The Army of the Potomac was bogged down in a war of attrition before Richmond, General Sherman was still a good distance from Atlanta, and to the average voter the end of the hated Civil War was nowhere in sight. Potatoes were $160 per bushel, cabbages were $10 per head, and gold was selling for over $270 an ounce. As Calvin Coolidge was to say in 1931 during the Great Depression, the country was "not in good shape."

Lincoln himself despaired of winning the coming election. "It seems exceedingly probable," he wrote in a sealed document for his cabinet, "that this Administration will not be re-elected. Then it will be my duty to cooperate with the President-elect, as to save the Union between the election and the inauguration, as he will have secured his election on such ground that he cannot possibly save it afterward."

Even Lincoln's political friends thought he was a misfit in the presidency. Said one Republican senator, "We went in for a rail-splitter, and we have got one." Another party leader declared that most Republicans were Lincoln men "from necessity" and were eager to "get a competent, loyal President, in the place of our present imbecile incumbent." Even a cabinet member—Secretary of War Stanton—publicly referred to the president as "a low, cunning clown," and Lockwood Todd, a nephew of Mrs. Lincoln, thought it "disgraceful" that Lincoln was in the family. He added that he "would not vote for him to save him from hell." Greeley reminded a Massachusetts senator of the theological book containing "Chapter One—Hell; Chapter Two—Hell Continued," and added, "That gives a hint of the way Old Abe ought to be talked to in this crisis."

A contemporary caricature of Abraham Lincoln.

To the Democrats, Lincoln was a spineless, imbecilic, "awful woeful ass," a "dictator," a "coarse, vulgar joker," a "grotesque baboon," and "a third-rate lawyer who once split rails and now splits the Union." Indeed, to hear the opposition tell it, the South seceded because of Lincoln's election, and if he were reelected, the South would fight on "for another thirty years."

The more extreme Peace Democrats were willing to allow slavery to continue if necessary to end the war, and they had many followers in the North. A speaker in Mount Vernon, Ohio, castigated Lincoln for continuing the war and "thus, even in the agony . . . of our national demise," flinging "away the hopes and interests of this nation." "God damn him" was heard in the crowd, amid laughter and cheers. And in the same town a farmer's wife would say repeatedly to her children, "Lincoln! how I loathe that name between my lips!"

The first nominating convention of 1864 was a rump convention of radical Republicans who thought that Lincoln was soft on the South. Its managers predicted a "giant mass rally," but only 158 faithful signed the register. The *Detroit Tribune* jeered, "Were the immortal 158 the masses? Truly answers Echo—Them Asses!" Be that as it may, the convention nominated as its presidential candidate John C. Fremont, a Union general and the Republican Party's standard-bearer in its first election try in 1856.

The regular Lincoln Republicans and the War Democrats formed an alliance, which they called the National Union Party. The *New York Herald* called them "a gathering of ghouls, vultures, hyenas and other feeders upon carrion [authorized by] the great ghoul at Washington." Their logic in supporting Lincoln, the *Herald* went on, was that he "had killed so many men he ought to be allowed another term to kill as many more."

The National Unionists held their convention in June. They nominated Lincoln and, as his running mate, Andrew Johnson of Tennessee, a War Democrat. Johnson appealed to Lincoln as one who would add balance to the ticket, but Thaddeus Stevens, the radical Republican Congressman, was incensed at the choice. "Can't you get a candidate for Vice President," he asked, "without going down into a damned rebel province for one?" Other Republicans thought Johnson was a "clownish drunk" and "dirty as cart-wheel grease," but Lincoln wanted him, and he was the choice of the convention.

Democratic newspapers didn't care for either member of the ticket, calling them such names as "a rail-splitting buffoon and a boorish tailor, both from the backwoods, both growing up in uncouth ignorance." The *New York World* called the nomination of these "two ignorant, boorish, third-rate backwoods lawyers" an "insult to the common sense of the people," and added, "The age of statesmen is gone. . . . God save the Republic . . . from the buffoon and gawk . . . we have for President." The *Chicago Times* reprinted the *Richmond Dispatch* editorial comment: "We say of Old Abe it would be impossible to find such another ass in the United States, and therefore, we say let him stay."

Lincoln said of his renomination, "I do not allow myself to suppose that . . . the convention [has decided] that I am either the greatest or best man in America, but rather they have concluded it is not best to swap horses while crossing the river." Many people were mystified, Lincoln said, that he would want a renomination, which "reminded him of a story." An itinerant preacher asked an official for permission to speak in Springfield,

Lincoln's hometown, "on the second coming of our Savior. 'Oh, Bosh,' said the official. 'if our Savior had ever been to Springfield and got away with his life, he'd be too smart to think of coming back again'"

The Democratic convention, or as the Republicans called it, "the Jeff Davis convention," nominated General George B. McClellan for president. Little Mac, as he was called by his friends—and also by his enemies, except that they accented a different word—accepted the nomination. He repudiated its peace platform, however, which called for the armies to cease hostilities and go home: The "Southern States would then be asked to join a convention to restore the Union." The question of what to do if they refused was not addressed.

Little Mac had been a thorn in Lincoln's side earlier in the war when he was the commander of the Army of the Potomac. He had a reputation for action but, to Lincoln's dismay, his commanding general continually prepared his troops to fight but never seemed willing to lead them into battle. McClellan's men did so much "digging in" that cartoonists depicted Little Mac with a shovel rather than a sword. "To fight is not his forte," Lincoln finally decided. Harry Truman put it in more descriptive terms a century later: "McClellan just sat on his ass," he said. The general's delays and excuses depressed Lincoln. To a friend's remark about the Army of the Potomac, Lincoln retorted, "So it is called, but that is a mistake; it is McClellan's bodyguard." On another particularly exasperating occasion, he wrote McClellan a note saying, "If you don't want to use the army I should like to borrow it."

Finally, McClellan engaged Robert E. Lee at Antietam in one of the bloodiest battles of the war. Had McClellan been more daring, Lincoln believed, he could have smashed Lee's army and ended the war, but his caution allowed Lee to escape. Instead of pursuing and destroying the Confederate army, McClellan regrouped and complained of "sore-tongued and fatigued horses." Lincoln, in a sarcastic reply, asked, "Will you pardon me for asking what the horses of your army have done since the battle of Antietam that fatigues anything?"

McClellan was not content to assume all the military responsibilities. He also insisted on giving Lincoln advice on how to run the government. Once after receiving one of McClellan's messages, Lincoln was asked what he intended to do about McClellan's attempted interference. "Nothing," Lincoln responded, "but it made me think of the man whose horse kicked up and stuck his foot through the stirrup. He said to the horse, 'If you are going to get on I will get off.'"

Lincoln ended McClellan's army career after Antietam. "I said I would remove him if he let Lee's army get away from him," Lincoln said, "and I must do so. He has got the slows."

The campaign of 1864 was fiercely fought and extremely dirty. The Republicans, considered underdogs at first, began the campaign by charging that all who had attended the Democratic convention were rebels or rebel sympathizers and that the convention and platform were treasonable. The considered opinion of the *New York Times* was that every man at the convention was a "black-hearted traitor." So successful was the Republicans' charge of treason that a contemporary historian wrote: "[the Democratic party] has the taint of disloyalty, which whether true or false will cling to it, like the poisoned shirt of Nessus, for a century." The historian's idea was right but his timing was wrong—the taint only lasted twenty years.

McClellan kicked off the Democrats' campaign with the statement: "The President is nothing more than a well-meaning baboon. He is the original gorilla. What a specimen to be at the head of our affairs!"

An anti-Lincoln biography was published anonymously, with the intention of making Lincoln look completely ridiculous. After giving a history of his early years and his political career, the biographer ended with this physical description: "When speaking [Lincoln] reminds one of the old signal-telegraph that used to stand on Staten Island. His head is shaped something like a ruta-bago, and his complexion is that of a Saratoga trunk. His hands and feet are plenty large enough, and in society he has the air of having too many of them. . . . In his habits he is by no means foppish, though he brushes his hair sometimes, and is said to wash. . . . He can hardly be called handsome, though he is certainly much better looking since he had the small-pox."

"[Lincoln] stands six feet twelve in socks, which he changes once every ten days," ran a popular description of the time. "His anatomy is composed mostly of bones, and when walking he resembles the offspring of a happy marriage between a derrick and a windmill."

Harsh criticism of Lincoln extended even to his Gettysburg Address, acclaimed today as one of the most beautiful pieces of prose in American literature. When it was delivered in a dedication ceremony in November 1863, it was roundly condemned. The *Harrisburg Patriot and Union* in its account of the day's activities, said, "We pass over the silly remarks of the President; for the credit of the nation we are willing that the veil of oblivion shall be dropped over them and that they shall no more be repeated or thought of." The *London Times* said, "The ceremony was rendered ludicrous by some of the sallies of that poor President Lincoln." The *Chicago Times* reported, "The cheek of every American must tingle with shame as he reads the silly, flat, and dishwatery utterances of the man who has to be pointed out to intelligent foreigners as the President of the United States. Lincoln cannot speak five grammatical sentences in succession." (The *Chicago Tribune*, however, observed, "the dedicatory remarks by President Lincoln will live among the annals of men.")

Lincoln was attacked repeatedly for his humor and depicted in cartoons as being a clown at the most inappropriate times and places. One cartoon in *Harper's Weekly* showed Lincoln facing Columbia, a forerunner of Uncle Sam, who is asking, "Where are my 15,000 sons—

Lincoln attacked for fabricated levity in the midst of Civil War horror. McClellan is administering to a wounded soldier and saying he would rather hear the ribald song "some other place and time."

murdered at Fredericksburg?" Lincoln is answering, "This reminds me of a little joke." Another cartoon showed Lincoln and his friend Ward Hill (Marshall) Lamon on the battlefield at Antietam, with dead and wounded men lying all around them. Lincoln is asking Lamon to "give us that song about Picayune Butler," a ribald song of the time, while McClellan interrupts his ministering to the wounded to say, "I would prefer to hear it some other place and time."

The Republican defenders were also busy. Most of them took the tack that McClellan himself was not a "traitor" like the Peace Democrats but merely a fool who was doing their bidding (like a man who "may not be a son of a bitch but he acts like one *all* the time"). "The imbecility of McClellan," one said, "will surrender [the country] to the traitors' hands." Others were bolder and lumped Little Mac in with the traitors: "It is true that their treason is more open and noisy than his, but his is nevertheless as real and earnest as theirs." A good number of the Republican attacks on McClellan were calculated to make him look ridiculous rather than malicious. One cartoon showed Lincoln holding McClellan (equipped with his standard shovel) in the palm of his hand and saying, "This reminds me of a little joke." McClellan's habit of stationing himself far behind the battle lines also provided ammunition for his detractors. So far behind the lines was he, one opponent said, that "in the retreat General McClellan for the first time in his life was found in the front."

Lincoln used wit as a means of bearing his burden, as on the occasion when a temperance advocate told him that General U.S. Grant, a tenacious fighter, was careless in his dress and drank to excess. "What are you going to do about it?" the man asked. "Find out what he drinks," Lincoln replied, "and send a barrel of it to my other generals." General Joseph Hooker, who succeeded McClellan, sent a dispatch to the president headed "Headquarters in the Saddle." "The trouble with Hooker," said Lincoln, "is he's got his headquarters where his hindquarters ought to be." A visitor to the White House once professed astonishment at finding Mr. Lincoln blacking his own shoes. "Whose shoes," asked Lincoln, "did you expect to find me blacking?" Lincoln, like all presidents, was accused of being two-faced, to which he replied, "Now I ask you, if I had another face, would I be using this one?"

McClellan with his shovel
reminding Lincoln of "a
little joke."

Both sides published a number of pamphlets in which biblical par-
allels were used for ridicule. The Democrats had one entitled *The Lincoln
Catechism* that put forth questions and then gave the answers. "What is
the constitution? A compact with hell, now obsolete. By whom hath the
Constitution been made obsolete? By Abraham Africanus the First. To
what end? That his days may be long in office. . . . Was Mr. Lincoln ever
distinguished as a military officer? He was, in the Black Hawk War.
What high military position did he hold in that war? He was a cook. . . .
Have the loyal leagues [the Republicans] a prayer? They have: Father
Abraham, who art in Washington, of glorious memory since the date of
the proclamation to free negroes. Thy kingdom come, and overthrow
the republic; thy will be done and the laws perish. Give us this day our
daily supply of greenbacks. Forgive us our plunders, but destroy the
Copperheads [Southern sympathizers]. Lead us into fat pastures; but
deliver us from the eye of detectives, and make us the equal of the negro;
for such shall be our kingdom, and the glory of thy administration."

The Republicans replied with *The Copperhead Catechism*. "What is
the chief aim of a Copperhead in this life? To abuse the President, vil-
ify the Administration, and glorify himself. What are the articles of thy
belief? I believe in One Country, One Constitution, One Destiny; and
in George B. McClellan, who was born of respectable parents; Suffered

"I Knew Him, Horatio, a Fellow of Infinite Jest," says "Hamlet" McClellan of Lincoln.

under Edwin M. Stanton; Was refused reinforcements and descended into the swamps of Chickahominy; He was driven therefrom by fire and by sword, and upon the seventh day of battle ascended Malvern Hill, from whence he withdrew to Harrison's Landing, where he rested many days; He returned to the Potomac, fought the Battle of Antietam, and entered into Oblivion; From this he shall one day arise and be elevated to the Presidential chair, there to dispense his favors unto all who follow him. I also believe in the unalienable doctrine of State Rights, And I finally believe in a Peace which is beyond everybody's understanding."

"Don't swap horses in the middle of the stream" is a neat political slogan, and it has been used by every incumbent president since Lincoln. What really got Lincoln reelected in 1864, however, was the drastic improvement in Union fortunes in the war. On September 3, when Lincoln's position looked the gloomiest, General William T. Sherman dispatched the message: "Atlanta is ours and fairly won." Shortly afterward came the news that Admiral Farragut had captured Mobile, after storming into Mobile Bay with the battle cry, "Damn the torpedoes. Full speed ahead."

"Sherman and Farragut have knocked the bottom out of the [Democratic] nominations," said Secretary of State Seward. Horace Greeley announced that henceforth his paper would "fly the banner" of Lincoln. "I shall fight like a savage in this campaign," he said, adding, "I hate McClellan." What a difference a few days made!

The Democrats continued to try, however, with slogans like: "Hurrah for Lincoln! And a rope to hang him!" "Time to swap horses, November 8th," "No more vulgar jokes," and "His election [in 1860] was a very sorry joke [itself]." The usual fun was made of his physical appearance. "But," replied the Republicans, "if all the ugly men in the United States vote for him, he will surely be elected!"

The election was held on November 8, and the result was decisive. Lincoln won with 2,213,665 votes, against 1,802,237 for McClellan. The electoral vote was a landslide: 212 to 21. McClellan carried only the states of Kentucky, New Jersey, and Delaware, prompting one partisan to say, "Behold! For Mac one full-grown pair of states, and also—Delaware."

The inauguration on March 4, 1865, was a great triumph for Lincoln. The war, for all practical purposes, was over, and Lincoln offered conciliation to the South: "With malice toward none, with charity for all, with firmness in the right as God gives us to see the right, let us strive on to finish the work we are in, to bind up the nation's wounds, to care for him who shall have borne the battle, and for his widow and his orphan, to do all which may achieve and cherish a just and lasting peace among ourselves and with all nations."

On April 7, 1865, Lincoln dispatched a message to Grant: "General Sheridan says 'If the thing is pressed I think that Lee will surrender.' Let the thing be pressed." Two days later, Lee surrendered and the war was over, but Lincoln was not to have the chance to "bind up the nation's wounds." On April 14 he was shot by an assassin while attending a play in Ford's Theater in Washington. He died early the next morning.

Abraham Lincoln had saved the Union. Once again the American political system had risen to the occasion and produced a great leader when less than greatness would have meant disaster. Secretary of War Stanton's words for the sorrowing nation are an eloquent and fitting epitaph: "Now he belongs to the ages."

The Stolen Election

A notable year in American history was 1876. It was the year the first electric lamp burned in Washington, the year General Custer wondered "where all those damned Indians came from" at Little Bighorn, and the centennial anniversary of the nation's birth. There was one other noteworthy event of 1876: It was the year of perhaps the only stolen presidential election.

There is some controversy about whether it was the only election stolen. Boss Thurlow Weed was heard to say, on the results of the 1856 election, "Buchanan's margin of victory was fifty-thousand dollars." The election of 1888, in which Benjamin Harrison ousted the incumbent Grover Cleveland, was also extremely close. In fact, Cleveland outpolled Harrison in the popular vote but lost the electoral vote. On the day after the election, Harrison expressed his thanks that "Providence has given us the victory." Boss Matthew Quay, a staunch party supporter, was infuriated by Harrison's innocent remark. Said Quay, "Think of the man! He ought to know that Providence hadn't a damn thing to do with it." He added, with candor, that Harrison would never know how many men "were compelled to approach the gates of the penitentiary to make him President."

And of course, the election of 2000 would become controversial as well, as we shall see.

The last year of President U. S. Grant's second term was 1876, and fraud and corruption dominated the headlines. Many felt that Grant himself was honest but acted like a "wooden-Indian President" who saw nothing, as scandal followed scandal, and grafters and thieves looted the treasury and debauched the country. Moreover, whenever a culprit was caught, Grant was the first to defend him. There were land grabs, salary grabs, whiskey frauds, banking scandals, mine scandals, and the famous Crédit Mobilier scandal, in which a holding company was set up with the stated purpose of building the Union Pacific Railroad, but with the real purpose of fleecing the government. One enterprising thief, the United States minister to Brazil, restive because he was remote from the looting at home, defrauded the Brazilian government of $100,000.

Grant plainly wanted a third term and therefore made statements to the effect that he did not want it. "Now for the third term," he said, "I do not want it any more than I did the first. . . . I would not accept a nomination if it were tendered, unless it should be under such circumstances as to make it an imperative duty." Both parties accepted this "declination with a string to it" promptly, with a House of Representatives resolution declaring that a third-term attempt "would be unwise, unpatriotic, and fraught with peril to our free institutions." Since the resolution passed by a vote of 233 to 18, Grant felt it wise to withdraw from the fray.

With Grant out of the way, the Republicans gathered in Cincinnati in June for their convention. The leading candidate was Congressman James G. Blaine of Maine, but he was tainted with the Crédit Mobilier and a host of other scandals. He had just "exonerated" himself of the Crédit Mobilier charges with what a fellow congressman called "one of the most consummate pieces of acting that ever occurred upon any stage on earth," when fresh corruption charges were made in connection with the Little Rock and Fort Smith Railroad Company.

Blaine also had the misfortune of suffering sunstroke before the convention formally got under way, and he had to be confined to his bed. His opponents naturally visited him and "had no hesitation in predicting that he would be dead within a week, or if not dead, utterly incapable of . . . bearing any strain," such as that of being president.

In spite of, or perhaps because of, these dire predictions, Blaine recovered and was put up for the nomination at the convention by Colonel Robert G. Ingersoll, the noted orator and agnostic. Ingersoll attempted to reassure the delegates on the moral issue by thundering that the Republicans "do not demand that their candidate shall have a certificate of moral character signed by the Confederate Congress." To illustrate Blaine's courage, Ingersoll christened him (if that is the phrase) with his famous nickname: "Like an armed warrior, like a *plumed knight*, James G. Blaine marched down the halls of the American Congress and threw his shining lance full and fair against the brazen forehead of the defamers of his country and maligners of his honor."

Some observers thought that if the balloting had taken place on the spot, Blaine would have stampeded the convention and received the nomination on the first ballot. Unfortunately for the plumed knight, however, Cincinnati, unlike Washington, did not yet have electric lights, and the supply for the gaslights was cut off suddenly, forcing an adjournment until the next day. One Robert W. Mackey later took credit for this act, but it is more likely that the real villain was Mackey's roommate at the convention, Matthew Quay. Boss Quay, it would seem, trusted nothing to Providence in this election either.

In spite of Ingersoll's eloquence, Blaine was stopped, and with the help of Quay and others, a dark-horse candidate, Governor Rutherford B. Hayes of Ohio, was nominated on the seventh ballot. One explanation for the choice of Hayes was that he was inoffensive, "a third-rate nonentity, whose only recommendation is that he is obnoxious to no one." This was the view of Henry Adams, a grandson of John Quincy Adams, who attended the convention. (He was also the author of *The Education of Henry Adams*, one of the great books of Western civilization.) When Joseph Pulitzer of the *New York World* was told that in an era of corruption "Hayes had never stolen," Pulitzer replied, "Good God! Has it come to this?"

The Republicans chose William A. Wheeler, by one account a "well-known" congressman from New York, for vice president. His fame, however, had not spread to Hayes, who whispered to an associate, "Who *is* Wheeler?"

The Democrats met two weeks later and nominated Governor Samuel J. Tilden of New York. In one way the choice was natural enough. The times cried out for reform and Tilden was the most famous reformer in the country, having destroyed the notorious Tweed Ring in New York. As one speaker said, a "reform campaign without Tilden would be like the play of *Hamlet* with Hamlet left out." As no one could imagine this, Tilden was chosen overwhelmingly. In spite of his reputation as a reformer, Tilden seemed a strange choice to many. He was sixty-two years old, in poor health, a rich corporation lawyer, and a bachelor ("He never felt the need for a wife"). These were unusual qualifications for a presidential candidate.

In the campaign, both sides, of course, called for reform. The Democrats enumerated the scandals of the Grant administration and promised to "throw the rascals out" (a common cry nowadays, but a new phrase then—borrowed from Horace Greeley, who had used it four years earlier in his unsuccessful presidential race against Grant).

"The Two-faced Tilden"
(A. B. Frost).

The Republicans praised their past performances but nevertheless were intent on improving them. To be on the safe side, they also waved the "bloody flag" of rebellion. Hayes's first order of business was a letter to Blaine, in which he said, "A Democratic victory will bring the Rebellion into power. Our strong ground is the dread of a solid South, *rebel rule*, etc. I hope that you will make these topics prominent in your speeches. *It leads people away from 'hard times,' which is our deadliest foe.*" Blaine was happy to oblige and stumped the country, waving the bloody shirt. A Republican Party worker in Indiana summed up the situation in his state: "A bloody-shirt campaign with money and Indiana is safe." He added that any other type of campaign and no money would be folly.

"Not every Democrat was a Rebel, but every Rebel was a Democrat," reasoned the Republicans. "Is it safe to trust the nation's affairs with men who had once raised their hands against her life?" Ingersoll was more eloquent: "Every man that shot Union soldiers was a Democrat! The man that assassinated Lincoln was a Democrat. Soldiers, every scar you have got on your heroic bodies was given you by a Democrat!" As for

Cynicism, 1876 style.

Tilden, Ingersoll said he was "a dried-up bachelor, as bad as Buchanan"—a damning charge indeed.

The first returns on election night indicated that Tilden had won. He had carried New York, Indiana, New Jersey, and Connecticut, as well as the "solid South," giving him an apparent count of 203 electoral votes to 166 for Hayes. "The new era begins," said the Democratic *New York World*. "Peace on earth and to men of good will is the glorious message of this glorious day." The Republican *Indianapolis Journal* sighed, "Tilden is elected. The announcement will carry pain to every loyal heart in the nation, but the inevitable truth may as well be stated." On the morning after the election, Hayes wrote his son, conceding defeat, and the following day, James A. Garfield, the Republican leader in the House and a future president, wrote a friend, "It now appears we are defeated by the combined power of rebellion, Catholicism, and whiskey, a trinity very hard to conquer."

Tilden would have been president, too, had it not been for the bumbling of a Democratic state chairman, who sent a message to the *New York Times* in the wee hours of the morning after the election, asking for the latest returns. "Please give your estimate of electoral votes secured for Tilden. Answer at once," he said.

Tilden had 184 sure electoral votes, and Hayes had 166, but three states with 19 votes—Florida, Louisiana, and South Carolina—were still out, though presumed from early returns to be for Tilden. It didn't take long for the *Times* editor, John Reid, a fanatic Republican, to add the 19 doubtful votes to Hayes's total to give him 185 votes and the election. "If they want to know the electoral vote," Reid surmised, "that means they are not certain they have won. If they are still in doubt, then we can go on from here and win the election!" The plot thus was hatched that resulted in stealing the election for Hayes.

Reid awakened the Republican officials and put his plan into action. He telegraphed south, "Hayes is elected if we have carried South Carolina, Florida, and Louisiana. Can you hold your state? Answer immediately." At the same time, Republican newspapers announced, "Hayes had 185 electoral votes and is elected."

The *Indianapolis Journal* apologized for its concession statement and noted, "the political situation has undergone a remarkable change . . .

trustworthy advices indicate almost unmistakably that Hayes and Wheeler are elected."

Prominent Republicans met with Grant the next morning, and although Grant's first impression was that "it looks to me as if Mr. Tilden was elected," he was prevailed upon to help. Reinforcements were sent to the army in the "disputed" states (troops were already there to police the elections), and "visiting statesmen" were dispatched "to watch the count," since, as Grant said, "The people will not be satisfied unless something is done in regard to it which will look like justice." (That is a correct quote!) As a precaution, Republican agents supplied with money were also sent south.

The Democrats were busy too. They had their own "visiting states-men," as well as men like Thurlow Weed, who offered to buy three members of the South Carolina election return board for $30,000. Tilden, however, refused to go along with Weed's plan, believing that "the fiery zealots of the Republican Party may try to count me out, but I don't think the better class of Republicans will permit it." Nor did Tilden agree to buy Louisiana or Florida, both of which were offered to him by Republican carpetbagger "recount supervisors," for $200,000 each. (In declining, Tilden noted that $200,000 "seemed to be standard.")

Hayes's first reaction to the postelection activity was to scoff. "I think we are defeated in spite of the recent good news," he said. "I am of the opinion that the Democrats have carried the country and elected Tilden. . . . I do heartily deprecate these dispatches." As the Republican effort got into high gear, however, he was willing to try. "I don't care for myself," he said. "The party, yes, and the country, too, can stand it; but I care for the poor colored men of the South."

Neither side was blameless in the election practices. As one historian noted, "It is hard to see any difference ethically between marching [illiterate ex-slaves] to the polls with marked ballots [as the Republicans did] and keeping them from voting by threats and intimidation [as the Democrats did]." Another said, "The corruption of one was as heinous as the cruelty of the other."

The issue, however, was not how the votes were cast but who had the most, and thus the Republicans had the job of "going behind the returns" to change the certified Democratic victories in the three states to

Republican victories. This they proceeded to do, "not flinching at the task." All the Returning Boards were composed of Republicans. In many cases, they simply threw out votes to change the outcome in certain boxes; in other cases they threw out entire boxes. In Precinct 3 of Key West, Florida, for example, in which all the residents were white, the vote was 401 for Tilden against 59 for Hayes. A bottle of ink was spilled on the certificate of the vote on the election night, though, and a new certificate was made the following morning. No allegations of wrongdoing were made, but the box was thrown out on the technicality that the new certificate was not made on election day.

Money and messages flowed south for five months while the dispute was raging. Furtive communications were exchanged, such as "Hold Florida and you have your own terms," "Be specific about how we will be taken care of," and "Send money. Danger great." Coded telegrams were used, such as "Robinson must go immediately to Philadelphia and then come here," meaning, "$3,000 must be deposited in the Centennial Bank in Philadelphia where I can draw it." Other codes were "Doctors plenty," meaning "Returning Board all right," "Cold reports," meaning

It nearly came to civil war (Thomas Nast).

"situation uncertain," and "South Carolina cotton high absolutely," meaning "South Carolina absolutely safe."

As a result of all these shenanigans, two sets of conflicting returns were sent from each of the disputed states, and a constitutional crisis developed. There was a real danger that inauguration day would arrive without a certified winner. The Senate, which was to announce the vote, was Republican, and the House, which would have to decide an election without a clear winner, was Democratic. "Tilden or Blood!" was heard in many quarters, and one newspaper said, "Tilden has been elected and by the Eternal he shall be inaugurated." The Republicans responded by noting, "General U.S. Grant, not Buchanan, is in charge of affairs at Washington." Grant himself observed that he "did not intend to have two governments or any South American *pronunciamentos*."

To head off the crisis, a number of plans were proposed. A Senate plan called for a commission to settle the dispute. It was to have an equal number of Democrats and Republicans, with an additional member chosen by lot from the Senate. Tilden had some understanding of the laws of probability and realized what the odds were of a Democrat's being chosen by lot from the Republican-dominated Senate. He therefore respectfully declined "to raffle for the Presidency."

Finally, the two parties agreed on a commission that would have fifteen members—five from the Senate, five from the House, and five from the Supreme Court. The ten House and Senate members and four of the court members were divided seven to seven between Democrats and Republicans. The plan was made acceptable to the Democrats by the specification that the four justices would select the fifth, tacitly understood to be Justice David Davis, who was thought to be friendly to Tilden's cause. As soon as the House passed the bill establishing the commission, however, Davis, in a strange and timely coincidence, was appointed a senator by the Illinois legislature, and the justices subsequently selected Justice Joseph Bradley as the fifteenth member of the commission.

The Democrats still had hopes, for even though Bradley was a Republican (there weren't any other Democratic justices at the time), he had a reputation for independence. Indeed, the rumor ran that Bradley, on the eve of the decision, had shown his opinion favoring Tilden to the Democratic national chairman. The chairman, however, left Bradley's house too soon. A number of Republican dignitaries spent the rest of the night with the judge.

The next day Bradley sided with the other Republicans on every count, and every disputed state was awarded to Hayes by an eight-to-seven vote. "It is what I expected," commented Tilden. "Fraud! Dishonesty! Corruption!" was the reaction across the country. "Lead us!

"Another Such Victory and I Am Undone" (Thomas Nast).

We will put you in the White House, where you belong," begged Tilden's supporters.

Hayes was declared elected, but taking his seat was another matter. The country was in an ugly mood, and many thought another civil war was imminent. "The judgment in effect exalts fraud, degrades justice, and consigns truth to the dungeon," cried one Democratic senator. A Louisville editor declared, "100,000 Kentuckians would see that justice was done." It was plain that a deal had to be struck with the South. "If we are saved," said Garfield, "it will be by the rebels."

So it was. Hayes, who had said his only concern was for "the poor colored men of the South," agreed to remove the federal troops from their area and (his enemies later charged) agreed not to enforce the Fifteenth Amendment, which guaranteed their right to vote. The southern Democrats thereupon dropped their objections to Hayes, saying, as Garfield reported, that "they have seen war enough and do not care to follow the lead of their Northern associates, who . . . were invincible in peace and invisible in war."

The deal, made two days before Hayes's inauguration, averted a major crisis. On inauguration day, Hayes's picture was shown in many leading newspapers, labeled with "Fraud!" across his forehead. The *New York Sun* appeared with the same black border it had used to announce Lincoln's death. Many other papers referred to the new president of the United States as "His Fraudulency," "Old 8 to 7," and simply "Rutherfraud B. Hayes."

Despite the fact that his election was stolen, Hayes was thought by many to be a "good and honest President." He ended Reconstruction in the South, weeded grafters out of the government, improved the civil service, and, as a popular saying went, "stood up for the church, the home, and the American gold standard." He is also remembered for his wife, who earned the nickname Lemonade Lucy by banning liquor from the White House. This extreme departure from the Grant era forced guests to resort to frozen rum punch, concealed in oranges supplied secretly by the servants.

A final touch was put to the 1876 campaign by the famous cartoonist Thomas Nast in March 1877. He depicted the Republican elephant bandaged all over, an arm in a sling, holding a crutch, with the caption, "Another such victory and I am undone."

Ma! Ma! Where's My Pa!

The only election to rival the Log Cabin Campaign for buffoonery was that of 1884. It had the added distinction of being, by one historical account, "the dirtiest campaign in United States history." According to their enemies, the candidates offered to the electorate were, on the one hand, "the town drunk" and "a coarse debaucher," and on the other, "an unrestrained public plunderer," who "had wallowed in spoils like a rhinoceros in an African pool."

It was the Gilded Age, the era of the robber barons, and a time when Mark Twain said that he could look at a congressman without awe, "even without embarrassment." Another writer said of the times, "the Standard [Oil Company] has done everything with the Pennsylvania legislature except refine it." Against this backdrop it must have taken a special kind of courage—or effrontery—for the chaplain to open the Republican convention with the prayer that "the incoming political campaign may be conducted with that decency, intelligence, patriotism and dignity of temper which become a free and intelligent people."

The Republicans nominated James G. Blaine, of 1876 fame, as their presidential candidate, in a "mass meeting of maniacs" (as the editor of the *Nation* called it). The nomination seriously split the party because of

Blaine as rhinoceros "wallowing in spoils" (Thomas Nast).

the wide talk of Blaine's "financial irregularities." (Some critics were more direct. In a preconvention cartoon he was labeled "rejected, too crooked.")

A reform group, known as the Mugwumps (they had their mugs on one side of the fence, some said, and their "wumps" on the other), refused to support Blaine and bolted to the Democrats. The Blaine Republicans called the Mugwumps "Assistant Democrats" and noted with contempt that they "had their hair parted in the middle, banged in front," and were "neither male nor female."

One of Blaine's enemies was the powerful New York political boss Roscoe Conkling, whose disaffection probably started in 1876, when Blaine referred to him as having a "turkey-gobbler strut" and likened him to "a dunghill." At any rate, when asked if he would support Blaine, Conkling, a lawyer, replied, "I do not engage in criminal practice."

In contrast to Blaine, the Democratic candidate, Grover Cleveland, was so honest he was "ugly honest," according to observers. He subscribed to the well-known but seldom believed statement that "a public office is a public trust," an extraordinary view for his time. He was

"The Presidential Recruiting Office," with Blaine rejected, too crooked (Bernard Gillam).

Grover the Good, and he remained incorruptible throughout his career, to the surprise and dismay of friends and enemies alike. Even the 1884 campaign did not change him.

In the beginning of the campaign, Cleveland's enemies could conjure up nothing on him viler than the charge that he was a "Presbyterian bigot" and a "cowardly bigot," though the terms probably were not meant synonymously. On the other hand, the Democrats and Mugwumps had a field day with Blaine's history of shady financial dealings. Blaine's friends affectionately called him the Plumed Knight (a name given him in 1876, as already noted, by Robert Ingersoll). But to his enemies he was the "tattooed man," depicted disrobed in a famous cartoon with "railroad bonds" and "corruption" written all over his body.

During the campaign a number of compromising letters regarding Blaine's business deals were discovered and published by the Mugwumps. Among them was one to Warren Fisher, a business associate, that was particularly damning. In it Blaine asked for a special favor and concluded with "Kind regards to Mrs. Fisher. Burn this letter." The Democrats now

"The Tattooed Man"—Blaine's corruption exposed in a takeoff on a famous painting of the time (Bernard Gillam).

sang and chanted: "Burn this letter! Burn this letter! / Kind regards to Mrs. Fisher." To the Republican rhyme "Blaine! Blaine! The man from Maine!" they answered: "Blaine! Blaine! James G. Blaine! The continental liar from the state of Maine. Burn this letter!"

The Republicans counterattacked by calling Cleveland a "lecherous beast," an "obese nincompoop," a "drunken sot," and in reference to his 250-pound bulk, "a small man everywhere except on the hay scales." Because as governor of New York he had not prevented the execution of two murderers, he was also dubbed "the hangman of Buffalo."

The worst for Cleveland, however, was yet to come. Ten days after the Democratic convention adjourned, the *Buffalo Telegraph* published an article with the front-page headline, "A *Terrible* Tale: A Dark Chapter in a Public Man's History," and the subtitle, "The Pitiful Story of Maria Halphin and Governor Cleveland's Son." Then followed the facts that Cleveland had had an illicit affair with the thirty-six-year-old widow Mrs. Halphin, who had subsequently borne a child. For good measure the *Telegraph* added that Cleveland was a drunkard and a libertine who had no business running for president.

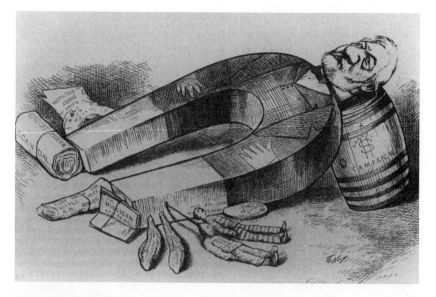

"Blaine, the Magnetic Statesman" attracts corruption (Thomas Nast).

The Republicans were exultant, and the Democrats were dismayed. What were they to do? they asked of Cleveland. "Whatever you do," he said, with characteristic honesty, "tell the truth," which must have demoralized his cohorts. The truth, Cleveland said, was that he *had* had an affair with Mrs. Halphin eight years earlier, and that although he was not sure of the child's paternity, he had contributed to its support. The boy was now growing up with adoptive parents. Mrs. Halphin was out of the public eye and refused to make any statements.

Ministers and reporters, however, made statements aplenty. Typical was the *New York Sun* article that read, "We do not believe that the American people will knowingly elect to the Presidency a coarse debauchee who would bring his harlots with him to Washington and hire lodgings for them convenient to the White House." Republican cartoons showed an infant labeled "another voice for Cleveland." Paraders chanted, "Ma, Ma, where's my Pa?" to which the Democrats replied, "Gone to the White House. Ha! Ha! Ha!" The Reverend George Bull of Buffalo declaimed, "The issue is evidently not between the two parties, but between the brothel and the home, between lust and law."

"Another Voice for Cleveland" (Frank Beard in *Judge*).

Cleveland was a regular Casanova, it seemed, for as the good reverend went on to say, "Investigations now disclose still more proof of debaucheries too horrible to relate and too vile to be readily believed. Women now married and anxious to cover the sins of their youth have been his victims, and are now alarmed lest their relations with him be exposed." The Reverend Henry Ward Beecher, however, defended Cleveland, accusing Blaine of "awhoring after votes." He said he would support Cleveland and that if every New Yorker who had violated the Seventh Commandment also voted for him, he would carry the state by 200,000 votes.

Fortunately for Cleveland, the Halphin affair broke early in the campaign. There was time for the voters to put it in proper perspective. Many agreed with the Mugwump who observed that Cleveland had great integrity in office but questionable credentials in private life, whereas Blaine was a model husband and father but was delinquent in office. He said therefore, "We should elect Mr. Cleveland to the public office which he is so qualified to fill and retire Mr. Blaine to the private life which he is so admirably fitted to adorn."

With a week left to go in the campaign, Blaine appeared to have a definite edge. This seemed to prove that charges of stealing went down more easily with the voters than those of drunkenness and illicit sex. In the last week, however, two events in one day destroyed Blaine.

The first blow was dealt in the afternoon by a preacher who, while trying to help, inadvertently proved to be Blaine's undoing. The occasion was a gathering of Protestant clergymen in New York who had endorsed Blaine, and the speaker was the Reverend Dr. Samuel Burchard. At one point in his rambling speech, the Reverend Dr. Burchard assured Blaine that the clergy were with him and that he [Dr. Burchard] and his colleagues would never support any candidate of the party of "rum, Romanism, and rebellion." New Yorkers didn't mind candidates running against rebels (after all, they had been doing it for twenty years), nor did they object, at least at that time, to swipes at drunks, such as they imagined Cleveland to be. But the Catholics among them did not take kindly to the slur against their religion. Poor Blaine was not really listening and thus did not repudiate the remark, thereby allowing the Democrats to make it seem that he agreed with the preacher. No one, in fact, seemed to notice the gaffe when it was made except a Democratic spy, who rushed to Democratic headquarters with the incredibly good news. "Surely Blaine met this remark," someone said. "That is the astounding thing," said the observer. "He made no reference to the words."

Overnight the Democrats printed handbills with "Rum, Romanism, and Rebellion," in bold letters and distributed them in every Catholic neighborhood in New York City. The handbills shamelessly implied that Blaine had approved the remark by his silence, and as usual in such cases, the impression grew that Blaine had made the remark himself. Blaine issued a disclaimer three days later, but the damage was done.

The second fateful event of that day was a dinner at Delmonico's Restaurant held for Blaine by a group of his wealthy supporters, including

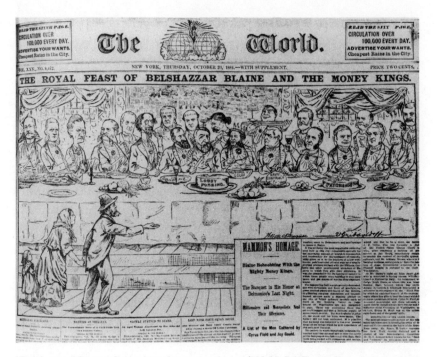

"Belshazzar" Blaine flanked by the money kings (W. H. McDougall in the *New York World*).

Jay Gould, John Jacob Astor, and Cyrus W. Field. The next morning the newspapers carried scathing editorial comments on the gathering, with front-page headlines like "The Royal Feast of Belshazzar Blaine and the Money Kings." A front-page cartoon showed Blaine and the millionaires at a table laden with terrapin, canvasback duck, and champagne, with a hungry family in the foreground begging for crumbs. The day, as the *New York World* reported, was "Mr. Blaine's black Wednesday."

As if all this weren't enough for Blaine, Providence sent a driving rain down on upstate New York on election day, which sharply reduced the Republican vote. Blaine lost New York by 1,149 votes, and with it the election. Outside New York the candidates were virtually tied (Cleveland, 183 electoral votes, and Blaine, 182), and so New York's 36 votes determined the outcome.

Because of the rains and the Reverend Dr. Burchard, Blaine later attributed his defeat to the fact that "the Lord sent upon us an ass in the shape of a preacher, and a rainstorm to lessen our vote in New York." Four years later the memory of Dr. Burchard still lingered in Republican circles. Their candidate, Benjamin Harrison, grandson of our friend William Henry Harrison of 1840, refused to leave his home during the campaign. "I have a great risk of meeting a fool at home," he said, "but the candidate who travels cannot escape him."

The irony of the dirty campaign of 1884 perhaps is that the candidate with the reputation for shady dealing and dirty tricks was done in by his supporters, Providence, and a dirty trick of his opposition.

President Cleveland was defeated in his bid for reelection in 1888. On March 4, 1889, when the new president, Benjamin Harrison, and his family were taking over the White House, Mrs. Cleveland cautioned an aide to keep everything in the house "as it is now, when we come back again." When the puzzled aide inquired when this would be, the outgoing first lady said, "just four years from today." This is precisely what happened, when Cleveland defeated Harrison in 1892, making Cleveland the only president to serve two nonconsecutive terms.

The Bull Moose Campaign

In America in 1912, the automobile self-starter was introduced, suffragettes marched on New York's Fifth Avenue, hard liquor was selling at six quarts for one dollar, Model T Fords abounded on the roads, there was no personal income tax, and the national debt stood at just eleven dollars per person. The year's best-selling novel was Zane Grey's *Riders of the Purple Sage*, and the popular songs were "Moonlight Bay," "Waiting for the Robert E. Lee," and Irving Berlin's "When the Midnight Choo Choo Leaves for Alabam." Sarah Bernhardt was starring in *Queen Elizabeth*, the first feature-length motion picture shown in America; the Boston Red Sox moved into newly completed Fenway Park; the Indian head/buffalo nickel was issued; a heart attack was first diagnosed in a living patient; and the fourth down was added to football. It was also the year the *Titanic* went down and the year of an unmatched presidential campaign, which saw a sitting president, a past president, and a future president in a three-way battle for the White House.

The incumbent president was Republican William Howard Taft, his challenger from within his party was ex-President Theodore Roosevelt, and the future president was Democrat Woodrow Wilson. In the language of the campaign, however, the race was between a "rat," "the most cunning and adroit demagogue that modern civilization had produced since Napoleon III," and a "long-haired bookworm of a professor."

The most colorful of the three contenders was Teddy Roosevelt, who to the dismay of Senator Mark Hanna had become president upon the assassination of President William McKinley in 1901. "I told McKinley it was a mistake to nominate that wild man [for vice president]," said Hanna. "Now look! That damned cowboy is President of the United States!"

TR had used the presidency as a "bully pulpit" and lashed out at the trusts and the "malefactors of great wealth." His motto was "Speak softly and carry a big stick," and he wielded his big stick freely. As he said of the building of the Panama Canal, for example, "I took the Isthmus, started the Canal, and then left Congress—not to debate the Canal, but to debate me." He was an exciting president and one of the few who seemed to relish the job. "No President has ever enjoyed himself as much as I have enjoyed myself," he said, on leaving office in 1909.

Roosevelt was elected to his second term in 1904, the only successful Republican candidate since Lincoln who was not a Civil War army officer born in Ohio (as were Grant, Hayes, Garfield, Benjamin Harrison, and McKinley). But on election night, after the results were in, TR made one of his few political mistakes. He said, "The wise custom which limits the President to two terms regards the substance and not the form, and under no circumstances will I be a candidate for or accept another nomination." He later admitted, "I would cut off my hand [at the wrist] . . . if I could recall that written statement."

In contrast to TR, Taft did not enjoy the presidency. "I have come to the conclusion," he once said, "that the major work of the President is to increase the gate receipts of expositions and fairs and bring tourists to town." On another occasion when someone asked him what could be done about unemployment, he replied, "God knows." When Roosevelt decided to make Taft his successor, he teased him by saying, "I have clairvoyant powers. I see a man standing before me weighing about 350 pounds. There is something hanging over his head. . . . At one time it looks like the presidency—then again it looks like the chief justiceship." "Make it the Presidency," cried Mrs. Taft. "Make it the chief justiceship," said Taft.

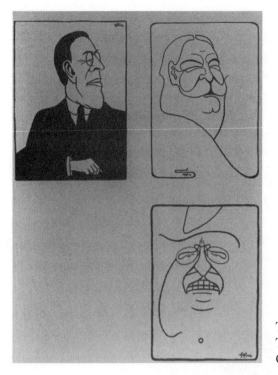

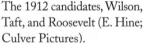

The 1912 candidates, Wilson, Taft, and Roosevelt (E. Hine; Culver Pictures).

At 330 pounds, Taft was the heaviest of all the presidents, and his weight was the butt of many jokes. A Supreme Court justice said that Taft was the politest man alive. "I heard that recently he rose in a street-car and gave his seat to three women." Senator Jonathan Dolliver of Iowa said, in criticizing Taft's presidency, that he was "a large body surrounded by men who knew exactly what they wanted."

Despite the jokes about him and his reluctance to be president, Taft was elected in 1908 with Roosevelt's help. On inauguration day, Washington experienced one of the nastiest blizzards in its history, prompting Taft to say to TR, "I always said it would be a cold day when I got to be President of the United States."

The third candidate of 1912, Woodrow Wilson, had his first experience in politics in 1860. "I was," Wilson said, "standing at my father's gateway . . . when I was four years old, and [heard] someone pass and say that Mr. Lincoln was elected and there was to be war." Wilson's first love was politics, but he took his doctorate and by 1890 had settled down to a professor's life at Princeton. When he finally decided to take up politics, his rise was "the phenomenon of all history." In September 1910, he was a college president who had never held a public office, and on March 4, 1913, he was president of the United States.

Wilson also had a biting wit. As governor of New Jersey he had a distressing phone call that a good friend, a United States senator from New Jersey, had just died. A moment later he had another phone call from a politician who said he "would like to take the senator's place." Wilson replied, "Well, you may quote me as saying that's perfectly agreeable to me if it's agreeable to the undertaker."

Roosevelt was only fifty years old when he turned over the presidency to Taft. He was at the height of his popularity and could easily

Taft as Teddy Roosevelt's heir apparent in happier times (Joseph Klepper; Culver Pictures).

have had the third term that he so badly wanted if it had not been for his rash promise not to run again. To drown his sorrows at leaving office, he plunged into the rough-and-tumble life of the outdoors. By 1910, however, he was having second thoughts about Taft. Either Roosevelt was getting the "itch to run again" himself, as his foes suggested, or he genuinely thought Taft was a mistake. "Mistake, hell! He was a disaster," said an editor who was friendly to Teddy. TR said that Taft "meant well, but he meant well feebly."

Taft was at a loss to understand Roosevelt's increasing hostility toward him. He had tried to please TR in everything he did and indeed tried to keep himself in Roosevelt's shadow. "When someone addresses Taft as 'Mr. President,'" a wag said, "he instinctively turns around to see where Roosevelt is." Nevertheless, relations between the two continued to deteriorate, and finally, upon his return from an African big game hunt in 1912 (during which his enemies prayed that "every lion will do his duty"), TR announced

The contenders, featuring Roosevelt as a thorn in Taft's flesh (Clifford Berryman; Library of Congress).

his candidacy. He did so by coining the expression, "My hat's in the ring," and added, "The fight is on and I'm stripped to the buff." He explained that his earlier promise not to seek a third term meant no third *consecutive* term.

At first Taft was genuinely grieved at TR's break with him. "Roosevelt was my closest friend," he said sorrowfully. But as Roosevelt continued to attack him as "disloyal" and guilty of "the grossest and most astounding hypocrisy," he decided that he had reached his limit. "I have been a man of straw long enough," Taft told the *New York Times*. "Even a rat in a corner will fight!"

Taft controlled the party machinery, but in 1912 presidential primaries were held for the first time in history, and TR used them to get delegates. By then Taft was resolved to keep Roosevelt from becoming president again, and he fought hard in the primaries. But a president who had called himself "a man of straw" and had compared himself to "a cornered rat" could not arouse the enthusiasm of the voters. This was especially true when he had an opponent like Roosevelt, who kept reminding the voters

"Forward!"—The Roosevelt-Taft split (Culver Pictures).

that Taft was not only a "rat in a corner," but a fat, sweating rat in a corner, at that. For good measure, TR added that Taft was a hypocrite, a promoter of fraud, an ingrate who would bite the hand that fed him, and a man "with brains of about three guinea-pig power." The results were predictable. Roosevelt won 278 delegates in the primaries to Taft's 48.

The nomination, however, was another matter. The Republican convention was held in Chicago on June 18, but the nomination was decided before the delegates convened. Taft's supporters dominated the National Committee, which ruled on the seating of the delegates. In one credentials fight after another, the committee ruled in favor of Taft. "There is no form of rascality which the Taft men have not resorted to," thundered Teddy to the press, but it did him no good. When the convention opened, Taft had 566 delegates, with only 540 needed for nomination, and Roosevelt had 466.

To counter what he called the "steam-roller" tactics of the Taft men—using another term coined in 1912—Roosevelt personally came to the convention. "It is a fight against theft—and the thieves will not win," he roared. Newspapermen asked if he was set for a tough fight. Did he welcome it? Was he in shape for it? "I feel fine," TR said, "I'm feeling like a bull moose!" And thus the name of the campaign was determined.

At the convention, on one vote after another, the Taft delegates were seated, while the Bull Moosers whistled "Toot, Toot!" and rubbed sandpaper together in imitation of the sounds of a steamroller. "We stand at Armageddon, and we battle for the Lord," screamed Roosevelt. In spite of the "stolen" delegates, the issue was in doubt until the end. Taft's men said they had a majority of forty, and TR's supporters said they had a majority of forty. What did it mean? "It means," chortled ex-Senator Chauncey Depew, "that there are at least eighty liars in the convention."

Warren G. Harding gave the nominating speech for Taft, calling him "the greatest progressive of the age," which must have infuriated Roosevelt. Harding droned on that Taft "was the finest example of lofty principles since the immortal Lincoln bore the scourge of vengeful tongues without a murmur from his noble heart."

When Harding's speech finally was over, the voting began. It was clear that Taft would win, so Teddy instructed his delegates not to participate. The first ballot result was Taft, 561 (enough to win), Roosevelt, 107, and

344 "present and not voting." "The only question now," said Depew, "is which corpse gets the flowers." "Chicago is a bad place to steal in," warned TR.

The Democratic convention was held a week later in Baltimore. A big question was: Would William Jennings Bryan be a candidate? "While life lasts," was the answer given by Democratic National Committee chairman Norman E. Mack.

The two chief contenders, however, were Senator Champ Clark of Missouri and Woodrow Wilson, who had moved from the groves of academe to the governorship of New Jersey. Clark was derided as the "patent medicine man," because for some reason he had signed a testimonial for "Electric Bitters," saying, "It seemed that all the organs in my body were out of order, but three bottles of Electric Bitters made me all right." He was ridiculed for the song his followers sang at rallies—the old "houn' dawg" song with the chorus: "I doan' keer if he is a houn', You gotta quit kickin' my dawg aroun'!"

Wilson, of course, was a "long-haired professor" with no business in politics. Not much more seemed necessary to add.

The *New York World* "had hoped that it would not be necessary to treat Mr. Clark's candidacy seriously. That was a compliment we paid to the intelligence of western and southern Democrats, but it was a compliment which we now find was undeserved." As ballot after ballot was taken, however, it was decided that Clark *was* a serious candidate, since he led by increasing margins on every one. On the tenth ballot, thanks to ninety votes from New York, Champ, in fact, had a majority. In those days, two-thirds of the delegates were necessary for nomination, but no candidate who reached a majority had ever failed to go on to the nomination.

At this point Bryan changed his vote from Clark to Wilson, on the grounds that New York's vote proved Clark was not a progressive. Some said it proved Clark might win before a deadlock could develop to result in Bryan's nomination. This slowed the Clark bandwagon somewhat, but it still took thirty-six more ballots to defeat him. Wilson was chosen on the forty-sixth ballot. It was predestination, said the Presbyterian Wilson. "God ordained that I should be the next President of the United States," he said to his astonished party chairman, who had expected to get some credit for it himself.

To run for vice president, the convention selected Governor Thomas R. Marshall of Indiana, famed for asserting, "what this country needs is a really good five-cent cigar." He also gets minor credit for this story: "Once there were two brothers. One ran away to sea, the other was elected vice president, and nothing was ever heard of them again."

Still unwilling to accept defeat and leave the political arena, Roosevelt and his group split from the Republicans and formed a new third party. They called themselves the Progressive party and held their convention in August. Roosevelt was nominated, to no one's surprise, and in his acceptance speech he declared that 1912 was the year in which the people had their chance to destroy the "rotting husks" otherwise known as the Republican and Democratic parties. The Democrats, he had said earlier, were "as stupid, bourbon and reactionary as ever before," and as for Taft, his "nomination was fraudulent." To suggestions that the Progressives compromise with the Republicans to keep out the hated Democrats, TR replied, "I hold that Mr. Taft stole the nomination, and I do not feel like arbitrating with a pickpocket as to whether or not he shall keep my watch."

One cynic called the Bull Moose platform "Roosevelt's Confession of Faith," and another said it contained everything "from the shorter catechism to how to build a birchbark canoe." The *New York Times* sneeringly called the platform a socialist document and sympathized with "poor Eugene Debs," the candidate of still another party—the Socialists—who after the Progressive raid had only "one university professor hereabout" still faithful to his cause.

The issues in the campaign focused on the big trusts and the high cost of living. Beef had not been so expensive in thirty years. At seventeen cents per pound, it was difficult for the average worker to buy with wages of two dollars a day. The Republicans promised the full dinner pail, and the Democrats promised tariff reform and new labor laws. Taft campaigned very little, figuring that he could not win but could keep Roosevelt from winning, which was his greatest hope. He was sorry that the Democrats, "an incompetent group," would take the election, "but the fear of Mr. Roosevelt's success made it necessary" to campaign. Wilson and TR campaigned vigorously, each considering the other his major opponent. Roosevelt knew he could beat Taft but was not sure about Wilson; thus

"An Irresistible Force Meets an Immovable Object" (Joseph Keppler; Culver Pictures).

his speeches, according to the *New York Evening Post,* were like those "Custer might have made to his scouts when he saw the Indians coming." As for the Taft-Roosevelt feud, Wilson pretended to take little notice of it, preferring, he said, the strategy of Napoleon: "Don't interfere when your enemy is destroying himself."

Despite Wilson's having called Bryan a demagogue in 1908 and wishing "that we could do something, at once dignified and effective, to knock Mr. Bryan once and for all into a cocked hat," Bryan was willing to campaign for the Democrats. This he did, as unstintingly as he had for himself, speaking ten times a day for seven weeks. One true charge he hurled at Roosevelt was that Teddy had stolen his Bull Moose ideas from the Democrats. "So I have," TR replied. "That is quite true. I have taken every one of them except those suited for the inmates of lunatic asylums."

What little campaigning Taft did was largely aimed at Roosevelt. He called him a "fakir," a "juggler," a "green goods man," and a "gold brick man," and said that by manipulation and deceit, "He is seeking to make his followers 'Holy Rollers.'" To his wife, however, Taft admitted, "Sometimes I think I might as well give up. . . . There are so many people in the country who don't like me . . . apparently on the Dr. Fell principle:

"I don't like you, Dr. Fell,
The reason why I cannot tell,
But this I know and know full well,
I don't like you, Dr. Fell."

Taft never liked campaigning and knew he was not good at it. The closest he ever came to complaining at having to do it, however, was when he marveled to an aide about how well McKinley had campaigned. "He was a born undertaker," said Taft. TR, on the other hand, relished being on the campaign trail. Once, however, he met his match when a drunken heckler kept interrupting his speech with shouts of "I'm a Democrat!" Finally Roosevelt paused and asked the heckler *why* he was a Democrat. "My grandfather was a Democrat, my father was a Democrat, and I am a Democrat," replied the heckler. Roosevelt then asked, "Suppose your grandfather had been a jackass and your father had been a jackass, what would you be?" The heckler instantly replied, "A Republican!"

Roosevelt fired much of his ammunition at Taft, such as when he noted several Taft badges in a crowd and observed, "they are the appropriate color of yellow." Taft's supporters replied in kind, with Harding comparing Roosevelt to Benedict Arnold and saying that he was "utterly without conscience and truth, and the greatest faker of all time." Another Taft supporter said of TR, "I wish I could believe he intended to do a single honest thing . . . if he were to be elected. I cannot." Still another, newspaper editor Henry Watterson, characterized TR as "as sweet a gentleman as ever scuttled a ship or cut a throat."

Wilson and Roosevelt also had a few choice words for each other. To TR's suggestion that Wilson should belong to his Ananias Club, named for a biblical character who was put to death for lying, Wilson countered that Roosevelt was a "self-appointed divinity," who had talked a good game of trust-busting but had done nothing when he was president. "There is no man who is big enough to play Providence," added Wilson.

Even Debs joined the assault on Roosevelt, chiding him for never having spent "a day in jail." Neither Roosevelt nor any of the others, continued Debs, "had ever been hit on the head by a policeman, or had produced enough to feed a gallinipper [a large mosquito]." Because Debs had had these experiences, his reasoning went, he could relate to working people. (Wilson would later help him relive these experiences by jailing him during World War I for the "treasonable acts" of criticizing Wilson's administration. Debs, however, was not deterred. He conducted his next campaign from his jail cell.)

Toward the end of the campaign there was a flash of drama, when an anti-third-term fanatic shot Roosevelt just before he was to deliver a speech. Physicians wanted to send him to a hospital, but TR refused to go. "I'll make this speech or die; one or the other," he said.

End of the Bull Moose Party (Edward W. Kemble; Culver Pictures).

"There is a bullet in my body," he told the astonished audience. "But it is nothing. . . . It takes more than that to kill a Bull Moose!" After the speech he was rushed to the hospital, where it was discovered that the bullet had first struck his metal spectacles case, which prevented it from going more than four inches into his chest wall, thus saving his life.

Wilson and Taft both sent telegrams of admiration and sympathy, and suspended their campaigns while Roosevelt was in the hospital. In six days Teddy was back on the hustings, to the amazement of his doctors, and the campaign went on.

On October 30, toward the end of the campaign, Taft's running mate, Vice President James Sherman, died, and an arrangement had to be made in case the Taft ticket received any electoral votes. Nicholas Murray Butler, president of Columbia University, was asked to take Sherman's place on the ticket, and he agreed, "as long as there is no chance of my being elected Vice President."

The Taft cow Pauline grazing on the lawn of the State, War and Navy Building (Library of Congress).

The election results were 6,286,214 votes for Wilson, 4,216,020 for Roosevelt, and 3,483,922 for Taft. The electoral vote was a landslide victory for Wilson, who received 435 votes to 88 for TR and 8 for Taft.

"The fight is over," Roosevelt said. "We are beaten. There is only one thing to do and that is go back to the Republican Party. You can't hold a party like the Progressive party together. . . . There are no loaves and fishes."

Taft was pleased with the outcome. He was out of the White House, which he hated, and Roosevelt was not in it. Taft, a good and honest man, will be remembered as a capable Supreme Court chief justice and as the last president to keep a cow in Washington.

Wilson, of course, went on to greatness as the nation's leader in World War I. He also brought the country an eight-hour working day, workman's compensation, and the anti-child-labor law, among many other things. He was the first successful candidate to stump openly (as we know it) for himself. He proved that a candidate could travel, shake hands, speak across the country, and still retain his dignity. He was also an idealist with vision, which, as one historian has said, is the reason Wilson's name still appears in the speeches of Democratic candidates, while no Republican has mentioned Taft for fifty years.

Hoover and Al

The election of 1928 was the last one in the Roaring Twenties, one of the most exciting eras of American history. Daring young flappers shocked their elders with their short skirts, bobbed hair, and free use of cosmetics and cigarettes. People flocked to hear the jazz bands play tunes like "Yes, We Have No Bananas" and idolized heroes like Charles Lindbergh, Rudolph Valentino, and Babe Ruth. In 1928 Henry Ford unveiled his new Model A, speculation soared in the bull market, where stocks had reached a "permanently high plateau," and because of prohibition, illegal drinking clubs, called speakeasies, were filled to capacity. Added to all this was one of our most colorful presidential elections, in which the main contestants were a mining engineer who was also a millionaire and a "dry" on prohibition, versus an unabashed "wet" Roman Catholic from the "sidewalks of New York."

The outgoing president was Calvin Coolidge, who was, in the words of the famous defense attorney Clarence Darrow, "the greatest man ever to come out of Plymouth Notch, Vermont," and who "looked like he had been weaned on a pickle," in the opinion of Alice Roosevelt Longworth, TR's daughter. Coolidge had assumed the presidency upon the death of Warren G. Harding in 1923 and was elected in his own right in 1924.

There was almost as much speculation among his fellow Republican hopefuls about Coolidge's plans for 1928 as there was in the stock market itself, but on August 3, 1927, Silent Cal tried to relieve the tension with the wordy (for him) statement: "I do not choose to run for President in 1928."

Ordinarily, this simple declaration should have settled the issue, but since it was a political statement, everyone wondered if it meant that Coolidge *did* choose to run. Herbert Hoover, the leading party hopeful, and "a fat Coolidge," according to the noted writer H. L. Mencken, looked up the word *choose* in the dictionary to see if it had any colloquial meaning peculiar to Vermont. Meanwhile Senator Charles Curtis, another hopeful, asked Coolidge for amplification, which, of course, he never got. Everyone would have known that Coolidge was serious if they had heard Mrs. Coolidge's remark, "Papa says there's going to be a depression." The great American humorist Will Rogers, said that he, Rogers, did not choose to run either, and actually wouldn't run under any circumstances, "no matter how bad the country needs a comedian by that time."

Hoover finally decided to bring the matter to a head. He asked Coolidge directly if he meant to file in the Ohio primary. No, said Coolidge. Would he mind if Hoover filed? Why not? said Silent Cal. Some months later, Hoover, still uncertain, offered Coolidge the 400 convention delegates he had accumulated, to which Coolidge replied, "If you have 400 delegates, you better keep them."

Prospects for victory never looked better for Republican hopefuls, if they could get rid of Coolidge. Money was gushing from the factories and pouring from the assembly lines, and "God was in His Heaven," as Mark Hanna had said of McKinley's better days. The only cloud on the horizon was farm prices, which curiously had slumped while industry was booming. To allay any fears on this score, however, Coolidge explained, "Well, farmers never have made money."

The Republican convention opened in Kansas City on June 12, with Coolidge's status still up in the air. The odds-on favorite, assuming no Coolidge candidacy, was Hoover, or "wonder boy," as Coolidge referred to him in private. The keynote address was long and so filled with praise that Will Rogers thought the speaker "was referring to Our Savior, till they told me, 'No, it was Coolidge.'" Will added, "The way he rated 'em was Coolidge, The Lord, and then Lincoln."

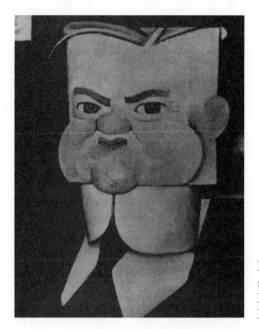

Hoover with his collar, a trade-mark of the caricaturist Charles Dunn (United Press International Photo).

There was at first a "Draft Coolidge" movement, which caused Mark Hanna's daughter to proclaim, "Hoover is done. That much is certain." This was followed by a demonstration by the farmers, who were pushing "anyone but Hoover." William Green, president of the American Federation of Labor, who was in town, called for 2.75 percent beer for the working man and a five-day week, in that order, and outside the convention hall, Kansas City authorities raided four bootlegging establishments.

In the end order prevailed, the Draft Coolidge movement died, and Hoover was nominated. For vice president the convention chose Curtis, who was to be the first Osage Indian in that exalted position. On the selection of Curtis, Will Rogers said, "The Republican Party owed Curtis something, but I didn't think they would be so low down as to pay him that way." Will had alerted the delegates earlier: "Dawes [Coolidge's vice president] is flying here to keep them from sentencing him to another four years."

In Hoover's acceptance speech he told the nation: "We in America are nearer the final triumph over poverty than ever before in the history of any land. . . . The poorhouse is vanishing from among us." As to the burning issue in the campaign, Hoover had written earlier to "dry" Senator William E. Borah that prohibition was "a great social and economic experiment, noble in motive and far-reaching in purpose." Thus Hoover seemed to be "dry," but he "was quiet about it." The "wets," however, shortened his description to Borah to "the noble experiment" and used it against him in the big cities. They kept quiet in the rural areas, which "would vote dry as long as the voters could stagger to the polls."

The Democratic convention opened in Houston on June 26, and there was never any doubt that the candidate would be wet Governor Al Smith, or Al(cohol) Smith, of New York. His name was put up for nomination by Franklin D. Roosevelt, who concluded his address with: "We offer one who has the will to win—who not only deserves success but commands it. Victory is his habit—the happy warrior, Alfred Smith." Roosevelt had nominated Al twice before—in 1920 and in 1924—which moved Will Rogers to say, "Franklin Roosevelt, a fine and wonderful man, who has devoted his life to nominating Al Smith, did his act from memory." He added, "You could wake him in the middle of the night and he would start to nominate Al."

Al was a proven vote getter and a formidable campaigner, but he had formidable drawbacks as well, especially in rural, small-town America. First of all he was wet, which many thought was enough to damn him to hell. In addition, he was a product of Tammany Hall, a city slicker from New York, and a Roman Catholic. Not even one of those characteristics had ever been found in a candidate for president, let alone all three! Teddy Roosevelt was the previous candidate nearest to a big-city man, and he got around this by proclaiming himself a rancher.

The Democratic platform was not wet, but it would have been difficult to say that the platform was dry. It pledged "the party and its nominees to an honest effort to support the Eighteenth Amendment [prohibition] and all other provisions of the federal Constitution and all laws enacted pursuant thereto." Smith, with candor reminiscent of John Quincy Adams, said he would as soon lose "as stand for something I don't believe in" and immediately sent a telegram to the convention outlining his views. The telegram called for "fundamental changes in the present provisions for national prohibition" and arrived just as the convention was adjourning, which probably was just as well for Al.

"The Sniper" (©1928 by the *New York Times* Company. Reprinted by permission.)

The official campaign followed standard lines. The issue, as the Republicans put it, was "Hoover and Happiness or Smith and Soup Houses? Which Shall It Be?" They promised "a chicken in every pot and two cars in every garage." Hoover said, "The slogan of progress is changing from the full dinner pail [McKinley's 1896 slogan] to the full garage." Republican cartoonists showed Al advocating "the full beer bucket." "The Republican Party," read an ad, "isn't a *Poor Man's Party*. Republican prosperity has erased that degrading word from our political vocabulary." Another slogan was "Let's keep what we've got. Prosperity didn't just happen."

The Democrats referred to Hoover as humorless and dull and repeated the Republicans' own preconvention jokes about him. "He smokes grimly," one said, which probably was funny to those who had seen him try. "Hoover asked someone to lend him a nickel," said another, "to buy a soda for a friend. 'Here's a dime,' was the reply. 'Treat them all.'"

To call attention to Hoover's long stay in England before joining the Coolidge administration and the pro-British labeling he subsequently received, the Democrats composed a song:

O 'Erbert lived over the h'ocean.
O 'Erbert lived over the sea;
O 'oo will go down to the h'ocean,
And drown 'Erbert 'Oover for me?

Both candidates used radio extensively, gave stump speeches, and rode in motor cavalcades. Charles Lindbergh endorsed Hoover. Babe Ruth was publicly for Smith. Al even appeared on television, becoming the first candidate to do so. General Electric broadcast his acceptance speech at Albany to its Schenectady plant fifteen miles away. The television set was described as a "strange, box-like contraption with a lens on front."

The unofficial campaign was vicious on the issues of prohibition and Smith's religion. The Ku Klux Klan did not build bunkers along the coast to keep the pope out, as Mencken suggested they would, but they did everything else they could think of. One example of their work was the publication of a bogus "Knights of Columbus Oath," which pledged priests to "wage war on Protestants and Masons" and to flay, lay waste, burn, poison, and so on.

Countless ministers did their moral and religious duties, too. In New York the Reverend John Roach Straton insisted that the Democrats, with Smith, had made "a covenant with death" and were "in agreement with hell." The Reverend Mordecai Ham told his flock in Oklahoma, "If you vote for Al Smith, you're voting against Christ and you'll all be damned."

"A vote for Smith is a vote for the Pope" was a tenet of faith with many voters. A typical flier showed Al at the opening of the new Holland Tunnel joining Manhattan and New Jersey, with a caption stating that if elected, Smith would extend the tunnel under the Atlantic Ocean to the Vatican's basement. A more realistic fear was that the pope would come by train, as an Indiana Klansman warned. "Watch the trains!" he cried. "The Pope may arrive in person on the north-bound train tomorrow!" A crowd gathered but was disappointed.

A Republican committeewoman in Virginia wrote a widely circulated letter stating that "Mr. Hoover, himself, and the National Committee are depending on the women to save our country . . . from being Romanized and rum-ridden." Hoover repudiated the letter immediately, saying that it "did violence to every instinct I possess." For the most part, however, Hoover wisely ignored the religious issue and the "political parsons."

On the lighter side, Al was accused of being a drunk, who required "two persons to hold him up" wherever he went. He was also called a Socialist, a charge that angered the Socialist candidate Norman Thomas, who didn't think Al deserved such praise. Finally, one well-known columnist alleged that Al's legislative record showed that he "favored prostitution as well as the saloon." The writer later admitted he was wrong and retracted the charge, because "a debate on the subject of harlotry was not worthy of a Presidential campaign." This praise and damnation attack caused another newsman to say, "None of the rest of us can put so much poison into a libel as he [Al's attacker] manages to leave in a retraction."

In one particularly hectic campaign rally at which the Happy Warrior was speaking, a heckler shouted, "Tell us all you know, Al. It won't take long." Al's quick retort was, "I'll tell us all we both know. It won't take any longer."

Smith was the best performer on the stump that the Democrats had ever had, with the possible exception of Bryan, and he gave his enemies hell in a manner that would not be seen again for twenty years, when Harry S. Truman did it. "Pour it on 'em Al, pour it on 'em!" responded his partisans.

A favorite gambit of Al's was to read and comment publicly on the Republican campaign literature. "Here's a good one for you," he would say. "'Republican efficiency has filled the working-man's dinner pail and his gasoline tank besides, and placed the whole nation in the silk stocking class!' Now just draw on your imagination for a moment, and see if you can in your mind's eye picture a man working at seventeen-fifty a week going out to a chicken dinner in his own automobile with silk socks on."

Mercifully the campaign finally ended. Hoover got over 21 million votes to Smith's 16 million and won the electoral vote by a margin of 444 to 87. Al was beaten decisively, but he polled the largest vote any Democratic candidate had ever received, twice as many as his party had gotten in 1924. Al also carried the nation's twelve largest cities, building the foundation for the great Democratic majorities of the next twenty years.

His enemies could quip that after the election Al sent a one-word cable to the pope: "Unpack"; but Al Smith had no reason to hang his

"A Bird in the Hand . . . ," the GOP with the full dinner pail, and Al with his full beer bucket (Jay N. "Ding" Darling; courtesy of the University Libraries, University of Iowa).

head. Indeed in one way he was lucky and the last laugh was on Hoover. As the columnist Elmer Davis said, "Adult Americans elected [Hoover] for the same reason that would have led Americans under the age of 10 to elect Santa Claus." But Santa Claus never came. Instead there was the stock market crash of 1929 and the Great Depression, and Calvin Coolidge was proved right for saying that when "people are thrown out of work, unemployment results." Herbert Hoover, a good and honest man, has had his name linked with hardship and disaster ever since. Coolidge summed up his bad luck: "If you put a rose in Hoover's hand, it would wilt."

The Only Third Term

The election of 1940, like that of 1860, was fought under the cloud of war. Europe was ablaze with World War II, France had fallen, and England stood alone against the madman Adolf Hitler. In America, Joe DiMaggio's batting average "slipped" to .352, and the New York Yankees lost the pennant for the first time in five years. The first Social Security checks went out, the first nylon stockings went on sale, and the first McDonald's hamburger stand opened in a drive-in theater in Pasadena, California. Two best-selling books were Ernest Hemingway's *For Whom the Bell Tolls* and Thomas Wolfe's *You Can't Go Home Again*, and Gene Autry popularized his new song, "Back in the Saddle Again." *Gone with the Wind* and *The Grapes of Wrath* played in movie theaters across the country, and a great debate raged over whether to give England "all aid short of war" or to build a "Fortress America" in which to withdraw for safety.

The biggest issue facing Americans, however, was the 1940 presidential election, which pitted a president running for an unprecedented third term against a man who had been a lifelong member of one major party but who was nominated by another. Never before had an incumbent president sought a third term, and never again would anyone do so, for in 1951 the Twenty-second Amendment, which prohibited a third term, was adopted. It is also safe to say that never again would such an unorthodox candidate emerge in such an unorthodox fashion as did the Republican candidate of 1940.

Franklin D. Roosevelt, the Democratic candidate and a fifth cousin of Theodore Roosevelt, seemed destined for the presidency from his earliest beginnings. His first brush with the office came at age seven, when his father, a staunch Democrat, took him to the White House to visit Grover Cleveland. "My little man," said Cleveland, patting young Franklin on the head, "I am making a strange wish for you. It is that you may never be President of the United States." Much later, when Roosevelt won his first election (to the New York State Senate in 1910), the Tammany boss Big Tim Sullivan, an enemy of Theodore Roosevelt, said of Franklin, "You know these Roosevelts. This fellow is still young. Wouldn't it be safer to drown him before he grows up?"

Franklin D. Roosevelt was first elected president in 1932, when Herbert Hoover was undone by what a J.P. Morgan associate called "a little distress selling on the Stock Exchange." Stocks lost 25 percent of their value in two days, one-third of the labor force subsequently became unemployed, and prohibition became a national joke. Roosevelt's New Deal was ushered in, despite Hoover's warning that with such an event "the grass will grow in the streets of a hundred cities, a thousand towns; the weeds will overrun the fields . . . churches and schoolhouses will decay."

The third-term controversy raged for most of 1940. No president had ever been elected to a third term. A few had tried for it, as was noted in the anti-Roosevelt (Theodore, that is) jingle of 1912:

> Washington wouldn't
> Grant couldn't
> Roosevelt shan't

As the year wore on, Democratic presidential hopefuls, other than Roosevelt, and members of the Republican Party grew more and more anxious about FDR's intentions. He persisted in refusing to reveal them. The Republicans were especially interested, since all the polls pointed

FDR with his tilted cigarette, a pose that infuriated his enemies (AP/Wide World Photos).

to 1940 as their best year since 1928, but if "That Man in the White House" chose to run again, all bets were off.

The chief Republican contenders were Senator Robert A. Taft, son of the late president, and Governor Thomas E. Dewey of New York. Dewey was a rising young star of thirty-seven, of whom Roosevelt's Secretary of the Interior, Harold Ickes, remarked that he had thrown "his diaper into the ring." Another Republican candidate, the darkest horse in Republican history, was Wendell L. Willkie, a rank amateur in politics. He was also a Wall Street lawyer and the president of Commonwealth and Southern Corporation. But even more damning, only a year or so earlier he had been a registered Democrat, who in fact had contributed $150 to FDR's campaign against Alf Landon.

The Republican convention opened in Philadelphia on June 1, two days after the fall of France and one day after the miraculous evacuation of Dunkirk. The platform was for "Americanism, preparedness, and peace," and it condemned Roosevelt for his "explosive utterances," which were "leading us into war." The controversial aid-to-Britain plank promised "the extension to all peoples fighting for liberty, or whose liberty is threatened, of such aid as shall not be in violation of international law or inconsistent with the requirements of our own national defense." H. L. Mencken said of this plank that it was "so written that it will fit both the triumph of democracy and the collapse of democracy, and approve both sending arms to England or sending only flowers."

Next came the nominations. Taft was qualified as a loyal Republican, who according to his wife had "brains, character, and experience." Dewey, as a white Anglo-Saxon Protestant governor of New York, was an excellent candidate regardless of his age or any diaper remarks from Ickes. As for Willkie, he was forty-eight, dynamic, with a sense of humor, and it was said that he wore long underwear. On the other hand, no less a dignitary than Harvey Firestone had told him years before that he would never amount to a great deal because "No Democrat can ever amount to much."

One of Willkie's managers had fretted for almost a year over how he could make Willkie look good to the delegates: "They'll ask me 'Willkie, who's Willkie?' And I'll tell them he's the President of the Commonwealth and Southern. The next question will be, 'Where does that railroad go to?' And I will explain that it isn't a railroad, it's a public utility holding company. Then they'll say . . . 'now we know you are just plain crazy.' And that would be without my even getting to mention that he's a Democrat."

All the candidates campaigned actively before the balloting began—especially Willkie, who defied tradition by actually attending the convention. One of the delegates he buttonholed was Senator Jim Watson of Willkie's home state of Indiana. "I admit I used to be a Democrat," Willkie said. "Used to be," snapped Watson. "You're a good Methodist," replied Willkie. "Don't you believe in conversion?" "Yes, Wendell," answered Watson. "It's all right if the town whore joins the church, but I wouldn't ask her to lead the choir the first night."

"We want Willkie! We want Willkie!" chanted his supporters. When the chairman tried to quiet them with the reminder that they were guests of the convention, they yelled back, "Guests hell! We *are* the convention!" Willkie's amateurs did everything right, even to the point of having a really spontaneous "spontaneous" demonstration. When Willkie was nominated, at first nothing happened on the floor! All the frenzy was going on in the galleries. Nobody had thought of plans for the demonstration. This was quickly remedied by a New York delegate, who tore that state's standard from the Dewey men and began parading around the floor. A small army quickly joined him, and an authentic demonstration took place for twenty minutes.

The voting began with Dewey in the lead on the first ballot. Taft was second, and Willkie was a distant third. Dewey faded with each subsequent ballot, however, and both Taft and Willkie gained. By the fifth ballot, Willkie was in the lead, followed closely by Taft, and all the others were out of the race. The sixth ballot provided Willkie with victory, and there was bedlam in the hall. Thus Dewey became "the first World War II casualty," as a wag said later, and the Republicans had themselves an "odd" candidate, who unlike Roosevelt, "calls wah, war, and fahmehs, farmers."

The Democratic convention opened in Chicago on July 15, five days after the Battle of Britain had begun. Vice President John Nance Garner, known as Cactus Jack, and Postmaster General James A. Farley were two of the announced candidates, but everything depended on FDR, who still kept his plans to himself. To his inquiring secretary, Missy LeHand, he said that "God would provide" a candidate. Miss LeHand replied that God had better get busy soon. The time was at hand.

Roosevelt started things off by sending word to the convention that he had "no wish to be a candidate again," and that "all of the delegates to this convention are free to vote for any candidate." This was followed by chants of "We want Roosevelt," "Florida wants Roosevelt," and—evidently by a Republican—of "Willkie wants Roosevelt." A picture of FDR was shown, followed by a demonstration lasting fifty-three minutes.

Even though Roosevelt "did not want to run," an anti-Roosevelt delegate, to be safe, introduced a motion that "no man should be eligible for a third term of the Presidential office." Since there were no women under consideration, and both Grant and Theodore Roosevelt were dead, the motion was interpreted as being aimed at Franklin D. Roosevelt, and accordingly it was overwhelmingly defeated by a voice vote.

An aid-to-Britain plank was adopted, which was similar to that of the Republicans, and a platform promise was made not to "send our army, naval, or air forces to fight in foreign lands outside of the Americas, except in case of attack." The nominations were made, followed by demonstrations for each of the candidates. Roosevelt's was the biggest and the longest, and it was done to the tune of "The Song of Franklin D. Roosevelt Jones." On the first ballot, FDR received nearly all of the 1,100 votes. The other candidates withdrew, and the nomination was made unanimous. Thus Roosevelt was "drafted" by the Democratic Party, and Willkie got his wish to meet the Champ.

The fight over the vice presidential nomination was more spirited, to say the least. It was understood that Garner would not be renominated, and that was fine with Cactus Jack, who later publicly declared the office as not being worth "a bucket of warm spit." (At least, *spit* was the word that appeared in the newspapers.) FDR made it known that he wanted Secretary of Agriculture Henry A. Wallace, a choice that was received with mixed emotions by the convention. "Henry's my second choice," said one delegate. "Who's your first choice?" asked another. "Any son of a bitch, red, white, black, or yellow, that can get the nomination," was the answer. In the end the anti-Wallace minirebellion blew itself out, and Wallace was nominated. One factor in his favor was a gracious speech to the convention by the First Lady, Eleanor Roosevelt. A second undoubtedly was FDR's statement to an aide: "Well, damn it to hell, they will go for Wallace or I won't run, and you can jolly well tell them so."

Willkie kicked off the campaign with an acceptance speech in his hometown of Elwood, Indiana. Before 200,000 people he accepted the nomination of the Republicans and then proceeded to shock their right wing by accepting also the major objectives of the Roosevelt administration. He "gave the Democrats hell," however, for their methods, denouncing Roosevelt for his conduct of foreign affairs and for courting "a war for which this country is hopelessly unprepared and which it emphatically does not want." "The New Deal has failed," he also said. He advocated the "philosophy of production" to replace the "philosophy of spending." (He stopped short of the harsh criticism of FDR used earlier by Louisiana's dictatorial senator Huey P. Long, who had broken with Roosevelt in his second term. Said Huey, "The Constitution guarantees

Willkie opening his campaign in Elwood, Indiana (AP/Wide World Photos).

us life, liberty, and the pursuit of happiness, but under Roosevelt, 1 percent of us have life, liberty, and happiness, and 99 percent have pursuit.")

Norman Thomas, who was still running as the Socialist candidate, described Willkie's speech as a "synthesis of *McGuffey's First Reader*, the genealogy of Indiana, the collected speeches of Tom Girdler [an anti-labor steel executive], and the *New Republic*." He accused Willkie of first agreeing with Roosevelt's entire program and then warning that it was taking the country straight into hell.

Some Republicans accused Willkie of endorsing the New Deal. One remarked, "every time Willkie opens his mouth he puts Roosevelt's words in it." Ickes called Willkie the "rich man's Roosevelt" and said that he made his acceptance speech at Elwood to convey the image of an Indiana farm boy rather than the "bare-foot boy of Wall Street." A Republican senator responded by calling Ickes a "Hitler in short pants."

Willkie replied that his office was "on Pine Street, a full block away from Wall Street."

"A vote for Willkie is a vote for Wall Street," one Democrat asserted. No, said others, "A vote for Willkie is a vote for Hitler." Thus the Democrats, who had been running against Hoover for twelve years, now added Wall Street and Hitler to their list of targets. As for Willkie, he was content to say, "A vote for Roosevelt is a vote for dictatorship." "Our democratic system will not outlast another four years," he stated, if "the third-term candidate" were reelected.

The issue of the third term was Willkie's strongest weapon, and he wielded it mercilessly. "The third-term candidate" has committed a "dictatorial" act, or "the third-term candidate" has committed an "act of war," he would say. When the Democrats accused him of falsifying Roosevelt's record, Willkie charged that the New Deal had still left 9 million men and women unemployed. "Mr. Third-Term Candidate," he said, "tell the American people if Wendell Willkie falsified that part of the record." Signs appeared at rallies saying, "No Third Term," and they were answered by Democratic signs of "Better a Third Termer than a Third Rater."

Willkie's oratory got out of control on several occasions, as when he said, "Roosevelt is the great appeaser. At Munich what was he doing? Was

"The Sphinx—1940 Model" (Leo Joseph Roche; Collection Franklin D. Roosevelt Library, Hyde Park, New York. Reproduced in the *Buffalo Courier-Express*).

he standing up, fighting for Democracy? Oh, no. He was telephoning Hitler, Mussolini, and Chamberlain, urging them to sell Czechoslovakia down the river." Then Willkie switched to attacking Roosevelt as a warmonger. "If his promises to keep our boys out of foreign wars is no better than his promises to balance the budget, they're already on the transports." He later issued a statement that he had "misspoken himself" on the Munich statement, but he stood by the other one.

Sometimes Willkie's flubs were more funny than shocking. In Cicero, Illinois, he began a speech by saying, "Now that we are in Chicago." Someone in the crowd yelled that he was not in Chicago, but in Cicero, to which Willkie replied, "All right, then to hell with Chicago."

The supporters of both candidates fired away at the opposition. Mayor Fiorello La Guardia of New York said that he preferred "Roosevelt with his known faults to Willkie with his unknown virtues." Replying in kind, a Republican said, "The President's only supporters are paupers, those that earn less than twelve hundred dollars, and the Roosevelt family." FDR replied with unrestrained glee that we should forget the Roosevelt family, "but these Americans whom this man calls 'paupers'" constitute half of the American people.

A Republican committeewoman wrote, "Heaven help a war, if it is going to be run by Winston Churchill and Franklin Roosevelt." Signs appeared at rallies reading "Willkie for President—of Commonwealth and Southern," and "We Don't Like Eleanor Either." Democrats used Lincoln's argument against changing horses in the middle of the stream, to which Willkie replied, "Well, for one thing, what are we doing in the middle of the stream?"

Hate groups were active, too. Some people said Willkie was pro-German, and others even called him a Nazi. "Once a German, always a German," said still another, referring to Willkie's ancestry. It was said that Willkie's sister "was married to a Nazi," and that Willkie himself was anti-Negro. Hitler's statement that "Negroes are apes" was quoted in a way that indicated Willkie agreed with it.

As for Roosevelt, his "real name was Franklin Rosenfield," and he was "President of the 'Jew'-nited States" and former "Governor of 'Jew' York." He was also a "member of the International Jewish Conspiracy"—but then so "was Willkie," who must have been the only Nazi in the organization.

"Mother, Wilfred Wrote a Bad Word!" (Reprinted
with permission from *Esquire Magazine*).

Willkie was even denounced as the "Candidate of Booze." A temperance publication carried the headline: "Every Booze Joint in the
U.S. May Be Headquarters for Willkie." The evidence cited was that
Willkie's two brothers were officials of the Seagram Distillers Company,
and that the candidate himself "likes a Scotch highball or two when he
knocks off from work."

Roosevelt's strategy during the campaign was to be "presidential" by
remaining at his desk and attending to the lofty duties of his office. "The
Battle of Britain could not be adjourned by Roosevelt," solemnly explained

Ickes, "in order to ride the circuit with Willkie." Roosevelt did engage, however, in a number of "nonpolitical speeches." In a political speech, he explained to Missy LeHand, one talks about politics, but in a nonpolitical speech the subject is government. Harry Truman was to say eight years later that he was getting ready to give a nonpolitical speech that was nonpartisan, but "one which the Democrats [of the area] will like to hear."

As the campaign entered its last few weeks, however, FDR scheduled five major political addresses. Some said he decided to campaign because the polls showed that Willkie had a good chance of winning; a few even showed him ahead. But most observers believed Roosevelt's statement, "I'm an old campaigner, and I like a good fight." Declaring that he was exercising his privilege of answering the "more fantastic misstatements" of the opposition, he lashed out at the Republicans in Congress who had tried to keep us unprepared and who had fought against aiding Britain. "Great Britain would never have received an ounce of help from us," he said, "if the decision had been left to Martin, Barton, and Fish [three isolationist Republicans]." Over and over he cited examples of Republican "faults," blaming them on "Martin, Barton, and Fish." Soon the audience got into the spirit of things and repeated gleefully with him the cadence, "Martin, Barton, and Fish," with the appropriate sneer on the last syllable.

In another speech Roosevelt spoke the lines, "I have said this before, but I shall say it again and again and again: 'Your boys are not going to be sent into foreign wars.'" His speechwriter wanted to add the phrase "except in case of attack," but FDR refused. "Of course we'll fight if we're attacked," he said. "If somebody attacks us, then it isn't a foreign war, is it? Or do they want me to guarantee that our troops will be sent into battle only in the event of another Civil War?"

On election day Roosevelt had 27 million votes to Willkie's 22 million and won by an electoral vote margin of 449 to 82. Some Republicans blamed the "reliefers," saying, "You can't beat Santa Claus." Others blamed Willkie for a "me-too" campaign. It is more probable that "Americans who were frightened of Roosevelt were more frightened of Hitler." None of these analyses, however, gives credit to the enormous confidence the people had in Roosevelt. As one historian said, "When Roosevelt said, 'My friends,' every listener believed him."

Willkie had no reason to feel ashamed of the result. He had fought a hard, skillful campaign, and even in his losing effort he received more votes than any Republican in history. Not until 1952, when Dwight Eisenhower won, did a Republican candidate do better. Willkie clearly had given the Champ the hardest fight of his three presidential election victories.

Roosevelt ran for president four times, against four different opponents. Of the four, Willkie was the only one he obviously both liked and respected. "You know," he said, "Willkie would have made a good Democrat. Too bad we lost him."

Give 'Em Hell, Harry

E very election is unique, but in some respects every election is similar to every other. The 1948 election, however, truly can be called unparalleled in the history of the United States. It was, for one thing, the biggest upset ever in American presidential politics. For another, the incumbent president was the underdog, a rare happening, and his overwhelming defeat was predicted from the beginning of the year right up to and indeed through election night by virtually every poll, every newspaper and newsmagazine, and every radio commentator. But in the wee hours of the morning following the election, as humorist Fred Allen put it, "The polls went to the dogs instead of the other way around."

In 1948 World War II had been over for three years and the country was enjoying one of its greatest periods of prosperity. There were 40 million automobiles on the nation's highways, long-playing records were new and everywhere, penicillin had come into its own as a miracle drug, the transistor was invented, *The Snake Pit* was one of the biggest movies of the year, "Your Hit Parade" and Bert Parks's "Stop the Music" were two top radio programs, Citation won racing's Triple Crown, and young Marlon Brando starred in Tennessee Williams's Broadway play *A Streetcar Named Desire*.

Harry S. Truman with the actress Lauren Bacall reclining on his piano (United Press International Photo).

Internationally, the Cold War was at its height, NATO was conceived that year, and the Berlin Airlift was ordered. Runaway inflation and the high cost of living were the domestic political issues. The Democratic president, Harry S. Truman, was blamed for the inflation, of course, but the Republican-controlled Eightieth Congress was also on the defensive. Price controls had been lifted largely through its efforts, and the cost of living had jumped 30 percent since 1946.

As the time for the national conventions drew near, the confident Republicans had a field day. "To err is Truman," they cracked. "Had enough? Vote Republican" was a popular slogan. The pollsters were certain of a Republican landslide no matter who Truman's opponent was. "The election must be held," one newspaper editorialized, "if for no other reason than to find out which national pollster comes the closest." From the beginning of the year until election night, no one thought Harry S. Truman would win—no one, that is, except Harry S. Truman.

The Republican convention met in late June in Philadelphia to nominate "the next president." Millions of Americans listened to the proceedings on their radios, and more millions in the Northeast watched through the new miracle of television. The leading candidates, as in 1940 and 1944, were Senator Robert A. Taft, now known as Mr. Republican, and Thomas E. Dewey, who was still the white Anglo-Saxon Protestant governor of New York and thus still formidable. Another major candidate was Senator Arthur Vandenberg, the leader of the Republican bipartisan group in the Senate. Vandenberg, formerly a staunch isolationist, had slowly converted to internationalism, a process Secretary of State Dean Acheson called Vandenberg's "long day's journey into our time."

At first General Dwight D. Eisenhower was sought out as a candidate, but he took himself out of the race because "being a general was not the proper training for the presidency," an observation that didn't do General Douglas MacArthur's presidential hopes any good, either. Some said that Ike's statement at a "private" dinner that inflation could be curbed if businessmen would "forego profits for a year" dampened his Republican hosts' enthusiasm for his candidacy. At any rate, the statement was "leaked" to the big-business circles, and Ike was reported as "disgusted" with politics.

Clare Booth Luce, a keynoter at the Republican convention, got things going with the observation that Truman was "a gone goose," whose "time is short and whose situation is hopeless. . . . Democratic presidents are always troubadours of trouble, crooners of catastrophe; they cannot win elections except in the climate of crisis." They thus have "a vested interest in depression at home and war abroad." Later Truman, accustomed as a Democrat to running against Hoover and the Great Depression, found it strange that the Republicans would mention the word *depression* in an election year. "You don't talk about rope in the house of one who has been hanged," he said.

Truman's other enemies found harsher things to say. He was "a squeaky-voiced tinhorn," Roosevelt's "ignorant successor," and in a speech of Taft's, simultaneously "friendly to Fascist groups" and "soft on Communism." Representative Charlie Halleck made a strange statement:

"There are a lot of people who find Truman is the poorest president since George Washington." There are a lot of others who find Washington was not so bad! Labor leader John L. Lewis said of Truman, "His principles are elastic. He is careless with the truth. He is a malignant, scheming sort of individual."

Dewey was nominated on the third ballot, and Governor Earl Warren of California was chosen by acclamation for the second spot. Taft had trailed badly on every ballot, because, some said, of the efficiency of Dewey's machine. Others blamed the chronic belief among many Republicans that Taft was "too conservative to win." A typical Taft philosophy that fostered this attitude was his "Let 'em eat beans" solution to the inflation problem. With the prices of meat so high, Taft said, low-income people could change their diets. They could eat less, or "Beans could be used [instead of meat] . . . to lower the costs of meals." "Low-income people" took to this like the businessmen took to Ike's suggestion that they forego their profits.

"A Good Man is Hard to Find"— Harry S. Truman with Dewey reclining on his piano (©Estate of Ben Shahn/Licensed by VAGA; New York, NY).

In nominating Dewey, the Republicans broke with a strong party tradition. They had never before nominated a candidate who had previously lost, as Dewey had against Franklin D. Roosevelt in 1944. The theory was apparently, as Alice Roosevelt Longworth observed, "you can't make a soufflé rise twice." Dewey won the nomination, according to columnist Max Lerner, "not because he had principles or even appeal, but because he had a machine [that was] . . . ruthless and well-oiled." He and Earl Warren proceeded to put this smoothly running machine in gear for a high-level, dignified campaign that they were certain would carry them to victory in November.

Amid placards reading, "I'm just mild about Harry," an unhappy Democratic convention, or as the *Detroit Free Press* said, "a quarreling gang of politicians" met on July 12, also in Philadelphia. Senator Alben Barkley noted in his keynote address that Dewey "proposes to clean the cobwebs from the government in Washington. I am not an expert on cobwebs, but if my memory does not betray me, when the Democratic Party took over the government of the United States sixteen years ago, even the spiders were so weak from starvation that they could not weave a cobweb in any department of the government in Washington."

Before the convention met, a number of futile efforts were made to draft first Eisenhower and then Supreme Court Justice Douglas for the Democratic nomination. On the first ballot, however, Truman was overwhelmingly nominated, no doubt along the lines of Teddy Roosevelt's theory about Charles Fairbanks's selection as his running mate in 1904. Said Teddy, "Who in the name of heaven else is there?"

Truman's vice-presidential candidate was Barkley, who was willing but said, "I don't want it [the nomination] passed around so long it's like a cold biscuit."

A fight developed over civil rights when young Mayor Hubert Humphrey of Minneapolis demanded that the Democrats take the party "out of the shadow of states' rights and into the sunlight of human rights." To Truman's surprise, the strong Humphrey plank was adopted, with the result that most of the southern Democrats walked out of the convention. The left wing of the party had already rallied around the third-party candidacy of Henry Wallace. Now the right wing split away, too, and formed a new party. A reporter told "Dixiecrat" Strom

Thurmond, who was to be the candidate of the southern wing, that Truman was only endorsing Franklin Roosevelt's past platforms on civil rights. "I agree," Thurmond replied, "but Truman really means it."

Newsweek magazine noted that before Truman's acceptance speech, "Nothing short of a stroke of magic could infuse the remnants of the party with enthusiasm. But magic he had; in a speech bristling with marching words, Mr. Truman brought the convention to its highest peak of excitement." "Senator Barkley and I will win this election, and make these Republicans like it," said HST to a standing ovation. To Barkley he said, "I'm going to fight hard. I'm going to give them hell!"

Everyone wrote Truman off as a loser. *Life* magazine showed a picture of Dewey with the caption, "The next President of the United States." The *Kiplinger News Letter* stated flatly: "Dewey will be in for eight years." Columnist Drew Pearson predicted that Dewey "will be a first-class President." Even Walter Lippmann, one of the most astute political observers of the time, believed that "The best the Democrats can hope for is to survive as an opposition."

Many observers could not hide their glee at Truman's plight. "He has a right to his light-headed opinions," said the *New York Daily Mirror*, "but he has no right to hold them and be President of the United States. The voters, according to all indications, will take care of the matter." "The Democratic plight has its comic quality," said the *New York Herald Tribune*, but warned the Republicans "to hold their laughter. The Democratic Party may be weak, but it does not follow that Mr. Truman is equally feeble as a candidate." As late as October 29, the chorus was the same. On that date the *San Francisco Chronicle* said, "It is a Godsend to this country and to the world at large that Harry Truman will get his dismissal notice next Tuesday."

Truman had a definition of what a presidential candidate should be: "First, he should be an honorable man. Then he should be a man who can get elected. Finally, he should be a man who knows what to do after he is elected." He believed he was a presidential candidate. It is one of the oddities of that odd year that everyone else discounted him, in spite of the fact that he was the same Truman who made the momentous decision to drop the atomic bomb, who saved Europe with the Marshall Plan and the Truman Doctrine, and who ordered the Berlin airlift and created NATO.

Wallace, Truman, and the "machine" Dewey kick off the campaign (Walt Kelly, in the *New York Star*, courtesy of Mrs. Walt Kelly).

A vintage Truman performance was the tongue-lashing he gave Soviet Foreign Minister Molotov when they were first introduced. "I have never been talked to in my life like this," said Molotov. "Carry out your agreements," replied Truman, "and you won't get talked to like this."

It was a strange election. Dewey campaigned like an incumbent against an upstart challenger. Truman seemed to be an out desperately trying to get in. Dewey worked the theme of unity and "moving shoulder to shoulder" toward some unspecified utopia. The polls told him that he needed only "to keep from losing," and so he was content to leave his audiences with such pearls of wisdom as "America's future . . . is still ahead of us" and "The highest purpose to which we could dedicate ourselves is to rediscover the everlasting variety among us," delivered at the Al Smith Memorial Dinner.

Truman traveled 31,000 miles and made over 350 speeches. He began with his acceptance speech when he castigated the "do-nothing Republican Eightieth Congress," and he announced that on July 26 ("Turnip Day in

Missouri") he was calling a special session to see "if there is any reality behind that Republican platform." The "do-nothing Republican Eightieth Congress" was his main theme throughout the campaign, but he also "poured it on" the "Wall Street reactionaries," the "economic tapeworms," and the "gluttons of privilege," who "stuck a pitchfork in the farmer's back" and "crudely and wickedly cheated" the people. "The Republican party," Truman said, "has shown in the Congress . . . that the leopard does not change its spots. It is still the party of Harding-Coolidge boom and Hoover depression."

"Give 'em hell, Harry!" the crowds would yell approvingly. "Well," Truman would respond, "I never give anybody hell. I just tell the truth and they think it's hell."

"The President is blackguarding the Congress at every whistle stop in the country," Taft said, which prompted the Democratic National Committee to conduct a "poll." The mayors of the "thriving, patriotic, modern, civic-minded, attractive, and prosperous American municipalities recently described by Senator Robert A. Taft (Rep. Ohio) as 'whistle stops'" were asked to wire the committee whether they agreed with

"Give 'em hell, Harry!" (D. R. Fitzpatrick in the *St. Louis Post Dispatch*).

Taft's description of their cities. A number of replies were received and duly published:

"Characteristically Senator Taft is confused, this time on whistles." (Laramie, Wyoming)

"Seattle is not a whistle stop, but everyone who sees her stops and whistles."

"If Senator Taft referred to Pocatello as 'whistle stop' it is apparent that he has not visited progressing Pocatello since time of his father's 1908 campaign for President."

"Senator Taft is in very poor taste to refer to Gary as whistle stop."

"The term hardly applies to the Los Angeles metropolitan area in which presently lives one thirty-fifth of all the people in the United States."

The polls continued to forecast a Dewey landslide. An exception was the Roper Poll, whose owner conceded the election to Dewey early in the campaign and announced that further polling was useless. The large, enthusiastic crowds that Truman attracted therefore puzzled the experts. Truman couldn't be taken seriously, in their view, so jokes and ridicule were used in place of explanations. "The President, in this critical hour," editorialized the *Washington Evening Star*, "is making a spectacle of himself in a political junket that would reflect discreditably on a ward heeler." A newsman observed, "With Truman's staff, Robert E. Lee couldn't carry Virginia." "How long is Dewey going to tolerate Truman's interference with running the government?" another asked.

An interesting detour occurred in Dewey's high-road campaign in Beaucoup, Illinois, when without warning his train backed up into the crowd. Fortunately no one was hurt—unless it was Dewey with the remark: "That's the first lunatic I've had for an engineer. He probably should be shot at sunrise, but we'll let him off this time." Truman needled, "Dewey objects to having engineers back up. He doesn't mention that under that great engineer, Hoover, we backed up into the worst depression in history." The irrepressible Harold Ickes, who had earlier labeled Dewey "the candidate in sneakers" (thereby promoting him from the candidate in diapers in 1940), added that the engineer had been listening to too many Dewey speeches in which Dewey wanted to turn the clock back to the days of Harding, Coolidge, and Hoover. "He honestly thought that Dewey wanted the train to run backwards, too." The noted columnist

James Reston simply observed, "the train left with a jerk." The engineer had the last word. On hearing of Dewey's remark he said, "That doesn't change my opinion of him. I didn't think much of him in the first place."

Truman's audiences were friendly as well as large. On one occasion a woman called up to Truman on the platform of his train. "You sound like you have a cold," she said. The crowd yelled its approval when Truman replied, "That's because I ride around in the wind with my mouth open." In September a newspaper publisher visiting HST in the White House, asked, "By the way, Mr. President, what exactly made you decide to run?" Looking around the room, Truman grinned and said, "Where would I ever find another house like this?" Toward the end of the campaign Truman told his audiences that he had a feeling he was being followed (by Dewey). He said he consulted his physician and was told not to worry. "There's one place that fellow's not going to follow you, and that's into the White House!"

Dewey continued to be "presidential," restraining his running mate Warren, who said he wanted to call *someone* an S.O.B. Meanwhile Truman pressed the attack. "We have the Republicans on the run," Truman said. "Of course, the Republicans don't admit that. They've got a poll that says they're going to win." These polls, he continued, were "like sleeping pills to lull the voters into sleeping on election day. You might call them sleeping polls." People should vote for him, he said "to keep the country from going to the dogs."

Finally the campaign, or Halloween, as Dewey called Truman's part in it, was over, and the candidates rested to await the outcome. Truman had changed the slogan from "mild" to "wild" about Harry, but still nobody seriously expected him to win. The *New York Herald Tribune* said, "Dewey has waged the most effective campaign of his political career." Drew Pearson said, "As a technician I would say Governor Dewey has conducted one of the most astute and skillful campaigns in recent years." The final polls showed Dewey certain to win. The major ones, Gallup, Roper, and Crossley, gave Dewey a lead of from 5 percent to 15 percent, and so did most of the state-by-state polls. Dewey was said to be leading in Iowa by 54 percent to 41 percent and in Illinois by 54.4 percent to 43.6 percent. The predictions of the *Fort Lauderdale Daily News* were so precise as to be carried out to two decimal places, with the astounding result of Dewey, 62.96 percent and Truman, 23.15 percent! Curiously the "feed bag" poll and the "popcorn" poll forecast a Truman victory, but these were "unscientific" polls in which livestock feed customers of an Omaha feed company and popcorn customers in movie theaters were allowed their choice of bags printed with donkeys or with elephants.

Surprisingly, the first returns showed no signs of a Dewey landslide. Truman was in the lead. Radio commentator H. V. Kaltenborn assured the country that "these are returns from a few cities. When the returns come in from the country, the result will show Dewey winning over-whelmingly." But as the night wore on, Truman's lead continued to hold. Jim Farley, on a national radio broadcast, reiterated what Kaltenborn had promised, saying Truman "cannot win, for when the reports come in from the country—the Dewey strongholds—his early lead will fold up." The *New York Daily News* in its early edition stated that Dewey was headed "for a popular vote margin and a possible electoral vote landslide."

At midnight Truman was still leading. At 5:00 A.M. Dewey said he was "still confident." But when daylight came, Harry Truman was the winner. At 11:14 A.M., after California and Ohio had gone to Truman, Dewey conceded. Truman had 303 electoral votes to Dewey's 89. Truman even carried Florida, and by a three-to-two margin, in spite of the prediction of the *Fort Lauderdale Daily News*.

In his own account of election night events Truman said, "At six o'clock I was defeated. At ten o'clock I was defeated. Twelve o'clock I was defeated. Four o'clock I had won the election. And the next morn-ing . . . in St. Louis, I was handed this paper [the *Chicago Tribune*] which said, 'DEWEY DEFEATS TRUMAN!' Of course, he wishes he had, but he didn't and that's all there was to it."

What went wrong? On election night one man told a reporter that political experts were like weathermen. "The weatherman predicted rain tonight," he said, "and the political experts picked Dewey. There's no rain, and it looks like it might not even be dewey."

Truman's folksy manner, aggressive style, and spunk undoubtedly were large factors in his victory. Seizing the Eightieth Congress as the telling issue was certainly the most effective single thing he did. The Republicans couldn't conceal their record, Truman said later. It was like Joe Louis said of one of his more elusive ring opponents, Truman added: "He could run but he couldn't hide."

The Morning After (United Press International Photo).

As for Thomas E. Dewey, he was an honorable man and a good campaigner who was lulled by the favorable polls into waging the wrong kind of campaign. As he said later, "The American people basically want a blood-and-thunder campaign."

Mr. Truman's place in history as one of our better presidents is secure. "He was right on all the big things, and wrong on all the little things," said his friend, Speaker of the House Sam Rayburn. As time passes, the big things loom larger and the little ones are being forgotten. Winston Churchill told Truman in 1952, "The last time you and I sat across a conference table was at Potsdam. I must confess, sir, I held you in very low regard. I loathed your taking the place of Franklin Roosevelt. I misjudged you badly. Since that time, you, more than any other man, saved Western civilization." HST will also be remembered as the gutsy president who gave us two great quotes: "The buck stops here" and "If you can't stand the heat, get out of the kitchen." Truman wrote his own epitaph when he said, "I did my damnedest, and that's all there was to it."

The New Frontier

The election of 1960 was in many ways the most remarkable election in United States history. Americans chose the youngest man ever elected president, forty-three-year-old John F. Kennedy, to succeed the oldest man at that time ever to hold the office, Dwight D. Eisenhower. The two major candidates were both born in the twentieth century—the first time that had ever happened; a Roman Catholic was the winner—another first; and the defeated candidate, Richard M. Nixon, was vice president with one of the most popular presidents ever, and still he lost.

In 1960 economic times were good. The fifty-star United States flag was unfurled for the first time. *Ben-Hur* won the Academy Award for best picture of the year. Ted Williams went into retirement with a home run on his last time at bat; Clark Gable made his last film, *The Misfits*; and in the news, a United States U-2 reconnaissance plane was shot down while assumed to be spying deep inside the U.S.S.R. The world was in the space age, the Russian *Sputnik* having been launched in 1957, followed by the American *Explorer* a few months later, in early 1958.

Not only was 1960 the space age, it was also the television age. In 1950 only 4 million American families had television sets, but by 1960 this figure had increased to 44 million (88 percent of all American families). In one respect, at least, the 1960 election was the television election. The two major candidates appeared face-to-face in four nationally televised "great debates," each with an average audience in excess of 65 million.

Kennedy was almost a campaign manager's dream of the perfect candidate. He had style and grace, and he was witty (on purpose, like Lincoln), handsome, well educated, and an authentic war hero. His PT-109 torpedo boat was wrecked by a Japanese destroyer in World War II, and Kennedy, the commanding officer, saved the engineer's life by swimming for five hours with the engineer's life-belt strap clenched between his teeth. He did face difficulties, however. The main one was dramatically illustrated early in the campaign by a conversation Bobby Kennedy, John's brother and campaign manager, had with a group of Kennedy supporters. After going over plans for one of the early primary fights, Bobby said, "Well, what are our problems?" A man jumped to his feet and shouted, "There's only one problem. He's a Catholic. That's our goddamned problem."

Nixon, on the other hand, had no religious problems, and he was well known, a vigorous campaigner, and the heir-apparent of the popular Ike. But he also had a flaw. Many considered his campaign tactics to be questionable, to say the least. Some thought he fit Margot Asquith's description of British prime minister David Lloyd George: "He could not see a belt without hitting below it." By 1960 Nixon had a reputation as a hatchet man and had acquired a nickname, Tricky Dick, which stayed to haunt him.

Kennedy knew that his religion and status as a relative unknown outside his home state of Massachusetts required him to enter every primary. To prove to party leaders that he could win, he had to win them all, and this he methodically proceeded to do. The issues, other than his religion, were his youth and his family's wealth. (His father was financier and ex-ambassador to England Joseph P. Kennedy.) To defend his age, he noted that he had more government experience than "all but a handful of American Presidents, and every President of the twentieth century—including Wilson, Roosevelt, and Truman," before their assuming the office. If age, not experience, was the standard, then a test excluding those under forty-four would have "kept Jefferson from writing the Declaration of Independence, Washington from commanding the Continental Army, Madison from fathering the Constitution . . . and Christopher Columbus from even discovering America."

As to his family wealth, Kennedy laughed it off. To charges of "buying elections," he said he had just received a telegram from his "generous Daddy" reading, "Dear Jack: Don't buy a single vote more than is necessary. I'll be damned if I'm going to pay for a landslide."

Kennedy also kidded about the religious issue, as when he said, "I think it well that we recall what happened to a great governor when he became a Presidential nominee. Despite his successful record as a governor, despite his plain-spoken voice, the campaign was a debacle." The listeners, assuming he was talking about Al Smith, would roar their approval when he ended with, "To top it off, he lost his own state. . . . You all know his name and his religion—Alfred M. Landon, Protestant."

All the members of the large Kennedy family pitched in to help in the primaries. In West Virginia, Kennedy's opponent was Senator Hubert Humphrey. Because the state was predominantly Protestant and thus critical to Kennedy, the family was extremely active. "They're all over the state," lamented Humphrey, "and they look alike and sound alike. . . . People think they're listening to Jack . . . in three or four different places at the same time."

The opponents of Kennedy and Humphrey hoped their contest would be "a good clean fight from which no survivors emerged," but Kennedy won an inconclusive victory in Wisconsin and a resounding one in West Virginia. After that Humphrey withdrew. Kennedy took the remaining primaries and was the clear Democratic leader as the convention approached.

Nixon, on the other hand, faced only one obstacle to the Republican nomination: Governor Nelson Rockefeller of New York. Rocky was cheerful, confident, intelligent, radiant, and rich ("I've never found it a handicap," he once said, "to be a Rockefeller"). He felt responsible for the welfare of the country. "I hate the thought of Dick Nixon being president of the United States," he said to an associate. Rockefeller discovered, however, that the more he actively campaigned, the more Nixon was kept in the limelight, and the better Nixon's chances became. Accordingly Rockefeller announced his withdrawal, adding that his decision was "definite and final," that is (according to a Rocky associate), until the convention. The direct-challenge method would not have worked anyway, the associate said, "except by driving a personal assault on Eisenhower."

The Democratic convention met in Los Angeles in the first week of July, with Kennedy the overwhelming favorite. Senate Majority Leader Lyndon B. Johnson was his principal opponent, with Adlai Stevenson a sentimental favorite of many of the delegates. Also opposed to Kennedy was Harry Truman, who backed Senator Stuart Symington. Truman thought Kennedy was too young, but mainly he distrusted the conservative politics of Kennedy's father. "I'm not against the Pope," Truman said. "I'm against the Pop."

When Adlai's name was placed in nomination, there was a lengthy and emotional demonstration for him. "Do not reject this man who has made us all proud to be Democrats," pleaded the speaker, Senator Eugene McCarthy, and roars of "We want Stevenson" went up from the galleries. The Kennedys were not concerned, however, because they had an accurate count of the votes. "Don't worry, Dad," John said to his father. "Stevenson has everything but delegates."

Kennedy was nominated on the first ballot, and the party closed ranks around him—a most unusual display for Democrats. Johnson sent him a message saying, "LBJ now means Let's Back Jack," and Truman said, "I'm from Missouri. He had to show me, and he did."

JFK's next order of business was to choose his running mate, and he surprised everyone by selecting Johnson, which caused an uproar and a near revolt among Kennedy's liberal friends. "What'll I say to all my friends in Boston," one said, "when they ask me why you picked Lyndon Johnson?" Kennedy smiled and said, "Pretend you know something they don't know." John Kenneth Galbraith, the great economist and friend of JFK's, helped smooth the ruffled feathers of the liberals with the observation, "This is the kind of political expediency Franklin Roosevelt would never have used—except in the case of John Nance Garner."

There was still the question of whether Johnson, the proud Senate majority leader, would accept an office referred to by its first occupant, John Adams, as "the most insignificant office that ever the invention of man contrived or his imagination conceived." Johnson's fellow Texan Sam Rayburn thought that without Johnson on the ticket, Nixon, whom he despised, would win the election, and he urged LBJ to accept. "I don't want a man who calls me a traitor to be president of the United States," Rayburn said. Johnson, of course, finally agreed to run, and many observers think his effective campaigning was the difference in Kennedy's subsequent victory. "The farther south he campaigned, the thicker his southern accent became," one said of Johnson.

In Kennedy's acceptance speech he coined the name of his administration. "We are not here to curse the darkness," he said, "but to light the candle. . . . We stand today on the edge of a New Frontier—the frontier of the 1960s. . . . Now begins another long journey. . . . Give me your help, and your hand, and your voice."

The Republican convention met in Chicago in late July. Ike had seemed lukewarm to Nixon's candidacy, noting to an associate, "The fact is, of course, I've watched Dick a long time and he just hasn't grown. So I just haven't honestly been able to believe that he is presidential timber." In January he announced that there were "half a dozen, or ten, or maybe a dozen, fine, virile men in the Republican party that I would gladly support." Finally in mid-March he endorsed Nixon, and so by convention time Nixon's nomination was cut-and-dried.

On May 1 Nixon had leaked to the press that Rockefeller was his choice for vice president, possibly to head off Rocky's presidential candidacy. Rocky publicly spurned the offer, however, as he did the honor of serving as keynote speaker. At the convention Nixon chose as his running mate the United Nations ambassador Henry Cabot Lodge, and his campaign strategy began to unfold. Nixon had just returned from Russia, where he had engaged in a "kitchen debate" with—and had pointed his finger at—Premier Nikita Khrushchev. Lodge had given the Russians hell in the United Nations at every opportunity. The Nixon-Lodge ticket would offer the voters experience and the ability to stand up to the Russians. In addition, they tried to live down the old Tricky Dick past with a new Nixon image and acted as if they had never heard of the Republican Party.

Kennedy and Johnson had to return to Congress, which was still in session, after the Democratic convention was over. There they plugged

"Seldom has a candidate had so much experience at not being responsible for decisions" (from *Straight Herblock*, Simon & Schuster, 1964).

for Medicare and other planks in the Democratic platform, but without success. Their real purpose was to get the session adjourned so they could take to the hustings. In the meantime Nixon was touring the Old South, explaining that southerners were not deserting the Democratic Party but that the Democrats had deserted the southerners. He received an enthusiastic welcome, especially in Atlanta, where his campaign was "the greatest thing . . . since the premiere of *Gone with the Wind.*"

Would You Buy a Used Car from this
Man? (author's collection).

The Democrats revived the old Nixon image with a glowering photograph of the vice president with the caption: "Would you buy a used
car from this man?" Kennedy said, "With all this talk about an old Nixon
and a new Nixon, it should be remembered that there was no old Lincoln
or a new Lincoln, no old Wilson or new Wilson, no old FDR or new
FDR. I cannot believe that the American people in these difficult times
will choose a man with this fuzzy image of his own political philosophy."

Nixon stressed that party labels were not important. "I believe," he
said, "that when we select a President of the United States that our history tells us that the American people look not just to party labels. They
look behind them." In contrast, Kennedy stressed party differences. "No
Democratic candidate," he said, "has ever run and said, 'Parties don't matter,' because we are proud of our record. We want to be identified with it.
We want to follow it." It was understandable, he declared, that Nixon
would not want to be associated with Republican "stand-pat" slogans and
candidates like McKinley, Harding, Coolidge, Hoover, Landon, and
Dewey. "Where do they get those candidates?" he asked his audiences.

Surprisingly, Kennedy encountered little heckling about his wealth.
At one stop he thought he was going to get it when a tough-looking
laboring man asked him if he had ever done manual labor for wages.
When Kennedy answered that he had not, the man replied, "Well, let
me tell you something. You ain't missed a damned thing!"

Nixon campaigned on his experience and attacked Kennedy for "downgrading America." He said the Kennedy program "would raise the price of everything the housewife buys by 25 percent." The program was too expensive. "It's not Jack's money he wants to spend, it's yours. . . . He may have more dollars, but you have more sense."

"We can do better. We've got to get this country moving again," was Kennedy's theme. As to experience, Nixon's meant nothing, he said. He quoted Oscar Wilde's remark that "experience is the name we give to our mistakes."

Nixon made the most of his "kitchen debate" with Khrushchev. Kennedy was "too naive and inexperienced to stand up to Khrushchev," he said, and chided Kennedy that he "would encourage Khrushchev and his fellow dictators to believe that this nation, the leader of the free world, is weak of will, is indecisive, is unsure of and hesitant to use her vast power."

"It is not naive to call for increased strength," replied Kennedy. "It is naive to think that freedom can prevail without it." He added, "Nothing I am saying will give Mr. Khrushchev the slightest encouragement. He is encouraged enough. The most ominous sound that Mr. Khrushchev can hear . . . is not of a debate in the United States, but the sound of America on the move, ready to move again." To his aides Kennedy joked, "Do you realize the responsibility I carry? I'm the only person between Nixon and the White House."

The religious issue was always present, of course, but it had its light-hearted moments, as when a Texas couple, visiting friends, were told, "I know you're anti-Catholic. I guess that means you're for Nixon." "We're not *that* anti-Catholic," was the reply.

More seriously, the president of the Southern Baptist Convention said, "No matter what Kennedy might say, he cannot separate himself from his church if he is a true Catholic. . . . All we ask is that Roman Catholicism lift its bloody hand from the throats of those that want to worship in the church of their choice." He added, "My church has enough members to beat Kennedy in this area if they all vote like I tell them to." The Reverend Dr. Norman Vincent Peale charged that a Catholic president would be under "extreme pressure from the hierarchy of his Church" to align United States foreign policy with that of the

Vatican. Reinhold Niebuhr and John Bennett of the Union Theological Seminary denounced Peale's statement, accusing him of having "loosed the floodgates of religious bigotry," and Adlai Stevenson said he found "Paul appealing and Peale appalling."

Kennedy, deciding to meet the issue head on, accepted an invitation to meet with the Greater Houston Ministerial Association. "I believe in an America where the separation of Church and State is absolute— where no Catholic prelate would tell the President (should he be a Catholic) how to act, and no Protestant minister should tell his parishioners for whom to vote," he told the ministers. "I am not the Catholic candidate for President, I am the Democratic Party's candidate for President who happens also to be a Catholic. I do not speak for my church on public matters, and the church does not speak for me."

The Houston speech impressed everyone who watched it, and though, as Kennedy told the ministers, "I am sure I have made no converts to my church," his speech probably made converts to his candidacy. "He ate 'em blood raw," said Rayburn.

In the middle of the campaign Nixon was hospitalized with a knee infection, and Kennedy decided to soft-pedal his campaign while Nixon was indisposed. He pointed out later at a news conference that he had promised not to mention Nixon "unless I could praise him, until he got out of the hospital—and I have not mentioned him."

When Nixon was out campaigning again, Kennedy was back on the attack. "Last Thursday night Mr. Nixon dismissed me as 'another Truman,'" Kennedy said. "I regard that as a great compliment, and I have no hesitation in returning the compliment. I consider him another Dewey."

The high point of the campaign was undoubtedly the "great debates." There were four of them, with the candidates face-to-face on national television. The first one, on September 26, was on domestic issues, and Kennedy opened it with his theme that the country could do better. He claimed that the economy was faltering, the country was stagnating, and our international position was deteriorating. We had to "get the country moving again," he said. Nixon was cautious in his reply. "Our disagreement is not about the goals of America but only about the means to reach those goals," he said. He contradicted a number of Kennedy's statements, but in general he agreed with more than he differed with.

The Great Debates (United Press International Photo).

The most devastating question put to Nixon in the first debate destroyed the myth of his superior maturity and experience. The questioner, reporter Sander Vanocur, recited a question put to Eisenhower at an August news conference: "What major decisions of your administration has the vice president participated in?" He asked Nixon how he could explain Ike's answer—"If you give me a week I might think of one. I don't know." Nixon's answer was that if you knew Ike "that was probably a facetious remark," but the question itself had already done the damage.

Kennedy was calm, confident, and ready with informed, forceful answers. Nixon was equally well prepared, but he was on the defensive and seemed less assured. On one occasion he said, "we must get rid of the farmer,"when he meant to say "farm surplus," and quickly corrected himself. The way he looked, however, was far more devastating than anything he said. Some said his face was made up—and it *was* in the succeeding debates—but for the first debate he had used only Lazy Shave powder to cover his five o'clock shadow. At any rate, he appeared "tense, almost frightened, at turns glowering and, occasionally, haggard-looking to the point of sickness," according to author Theodore White. Ironically, the radio audience thought the vice president won the debate, supporting the notion that Nixon's looks undid him instead of what he said.

In the third debate the question of Truman's profane language in the campaign was raised. Kennedy, to whom the question was directed, shrugged it off as a joke, saying that Mrs. Truman could get the ex-president to change, "but I know I can't." Nixon, however, had a detailed response: "One thing I have noted as I have traveled around the country are [*sic*] the tremendous number of children who come out to see the presidential candidates . . . mothers holding their babies up. . . . It makes you realize that whoever is president is going to be a man that all the children of America will either look up to or look down to. . . . And I only hope that, should I win this election . . . whenever any mother or father talks to his child, he can look at the man in the White House [with respect]." (It is ironic that Mr. Nixon, who was so concerned about clean language in 1960, was recorded on the Watergate tapes released in 1973 and 1974 in conversations containing one vulgarity after another. In the published transcripts of the tapes the vulgarities were replaced by "expletive deleted," a phrase that appeared so often it became a national joke.)

As the campaign progressed, particularly after the first debate, Kennedy became more confident and kidded with the crowds. In one talk, speaking hurriedly, he repeated the same phrase three times in one sentence, to the amusement of the crowd. Kennedy also laughed and said, "We're going to put this speech to music and make a fortune out of it." Speaking to a group of Iowa farmers, he expressed concern for their economic problems by asking in his Cape Cod accent, "What's wrong with the American fah-mah today?" As he paused for effect, someone in the audience answered, "He's stah-ving!" His listeners roared with laughter, and so did Kennedy.

At the Al Smith Memorial Dinner, which Nixon also attended, Kennedy was in rare form. He expressed pleasure that the dinner "could bring together amicably, at the same banquet table, for the first time in this campaign, two political leaders who are increasingly apprehensive about the November election—who have long eyed each other suspiciously and who have disagreed so strongly, both publicly and privately—Vice President Nixon and Governor Rockefeller." He continued with the observation that "the worst news for the Republicans this week was that Casey Stengel has been fired. It must show that experience does not count." Stengel had managed the New York Yankees, with ten pennants in twelve years—including 1960.

Kennedy concluded with a remark about Truman's use of profanity in the campaign. "I have sent him the following note: 'Dear Mr. President: I have noted with interest your suggestion as to where those who vote for my opponent should go. While I understand and sympathize with your deep motivation, I think it is important that our side try to refrain from raising the religious issue.'"

Toward the end of the campaign Nixon, sensing that he was in trouble, reverted to harsher language. "In the last seven days," remarked Kennedy, "he has called me an ignoramus, a liar, a Pied Piper, and all the rest. I just confine myself to calling him a Republican . . . and he says that is really getting low." Nixon also accused Kennedy of telling "a barefaced lie" about the Republican stand on Social Security. To this Kennedy replied, "Having seen him four times close up . . . and made up, I would not accuse Mr. Nixon of being barefaced, but the American people can determine who is telling the truth."

The polls showed Kennedy in the lead after the debates, but in the last week Eisenhower joined Nixon's campaign. Curiously, he had not been asked to do so earlier. "All we want out of Ike," said one Nixonite, "is for him to handle Khrushchev at the U.N. and not let things blow up there. That's *all!*" Ike's last-minute appeals were, in Nixon's words, "the most hard-hitting political speeches" the president ever made. The last poll showed the candidates in a virtual tie, prompting comedian Mort Sahl to quip, "Neither candidate is going to win."

Although Ike's intervention hurt, Kennedy had little choice but to kid about it. Why did Nixon need Ike, Lodge, and Rockefeller, Kennedy wondered to his audiences, "to escort him through New York?" Why did he "not add Dewey, Hoover, and Landon?" or "get [conservative Senator] Barry Goldwater out of that Confederate uniform that he has been using in the South . . . and get him up North?"

On his own triumphal night in New York City, which attracted a crowd of 1,250,000, Kennedy called the Eisenhower-Nixon tour "Nixon Day in New York," and said it reminded him of "those elephants in the circus. They have their heads of ivory, thick skin, no vision, long memory, and when they move around the ring in the circus, they grab the tail of the elephant in front of them. Well, Dick grabbed that tail in 1952 and 1956, but in 1960 he is running, not the President. . . . I stand tonight where Woodrow Wilson stood, and Franklin Roosevelt stood, and Harry Truman stood. Dick Nixon stands where McKinley stood and Taft—listen to these candidates—Harding, Coolidge, Landon, Dewey. Where do they get them?"

In the last days of the campaign, Nixon promised, if elected, to go to Eastern Europe "to carry the message of freedom into the Communist world." When that idea failed to arouse interest, he proposed, on the day

The Torch Is Passed—Eisenhower and Kennedy at the inauguration (United Press International Photo).

Lincoln mourns by Bill Mauldin (November 1963). Reprinted with special permission from the Chicago Sun-Times, Inc. © 2003.

before the election, to send Eisenhower. Ike suggested that Hoover and Truman also go to make it a nonpartisan mission. Truman declined, saying such a thing "should have been done seven years ago." Kennedy's response was, "If I'm elected, I'm going to Washington, D.C., and get this country moving again."

Kennedy spent the last day before the election in New England, and he confined himself to serious discussions. In Connecticut he said, "At the time of the American Revolution, Thomas Paine said the cause of America is the cause of all mankind. Now in 1960 the cause of all mankind is the cause of America." He closed his speech with a quotation "which Lincoln wrote in a campaign very much like this, one hundred years ago. . . . 'I know there is a God, and I know He hates injustice. I see the storm coming and I know His hand is in it. But if He has a place and a part for me, I believe that I am ready.' Now, a hundred years later . . . if He has a place and a part for me, I believe that *we* are ready."

Kennedy was elected with 303 electoral votes to Nixon's 219, but the election was one of the closest in history. Kennedy's popular vote margin was only 112,881 out of over 68 million. A shift of 37,000 votes in Illinois and Texas would have changed the result. Nixon waited until morning to concede, hoping for "a similar but reverse situation" to that of Charles Evans Hughes in 1916. Hughes had retired on election night, thinking he had defeated Woodrow Wilson. During the night the late returns from California reversed the outcome, and a reporter calling on Hughes the next day was told, "The President is sleeping." "Well," said the reporter, "when he wakes up, tell him he isn't President."

Nixon publicly did not seem to question the close election, as he might have been expected to do. He didn't even go as far as Richard Tuck—a defeated candidate in a later California senatorial race, who said, "The people have spoken—the bastards." Instead, his people conducted a covert check of a number of precincts and concluded that he had indeed lost, after which he made a gracious concession speech.

The inaugural address was memorable. "Let the word go forth from this time and place, to friend and foe alike," Kennedy proclaimed, "that the torch has been passed to a new generation of Americans—born in this century, tempered by war, disciplined by a hard and bitter peace, proud of our ancient heritage—and unwilling to witness or permit the slow undoing of those human rights to which this nation has always been committed." He continued, defining the tasks facing the country and noting that they "will not be finished in the first hundred days . . . nor in the first thousand days, nor in the life of this administration, nor perhaps in our lifetime on this planet. But let us begin."

But a thousand days was all John Kennedy had before the senseless, evil act that took his life on November 22, 1963. His presidency was brief, and his critics say it was "more style than substance." To his admirers, however, JFK's tenure is like the legendary Camelot described in the lines of his favorite song about King Arthur and his followers. Shortly after he died, his wife, Jacqueline, made an observation with which most of John F. Kennedy's admirers would agree. She said, "There'll be great presidents again, but there'll never be another Camelot."

Watergate

The story of the era from 1960 to 1980 is in many respects the saga of Richard Nixon—one of the most interesting in American presidential politics. From 1952 to 1974 Nixon figured prominently in every national election, running for president three times, for vice president twice, and appearing as a top Republican spokesman in off-year elections. His Watergate scandal, the worst in the history of the presidency, made Gerald Ford president, and by making the voters suspicious of establishment politicians, made possible the emergence of a rank outsider, Jimmy Carter, as the successful challenger in 1976.

Nixon had a checkered career, careening from one crisis to another in the manner of an alcoholic, charging his opponents with smearing him and being charged by them with lying, deceitfulness, and trickery. It all began in 1946, when he appeared before a California group of businessmen in response to their newspaper ad seeking a candidate for Congress. He spoke of the American system of "government control" of our lives "advocated by the New Deal" as opposed to one that "calls for individual freedoms and all that initiative can produce." Concluding, he said, "I hold with the latter viewpoint. I believe the returning veterans—

and I have talked to many of them in the foxholes—will not be satisfied with a dole or a government handout."

Nixon served in the Navy, in the rear echelons of the Pacific, and could never have seen a foxhole in the first place, as noted by author Frank Mankiewicz. In the second place, Mankiewicz asked, Would a man in a foxhole be entertaining guests? And discussing economic philosophies? These questions undoubtedly occurred to the California group, as well, but still they endorsed Nixon, presumably because of his brazenness, thus launching his career.

The late forties and early fifties was a sordid era in American politics, when many second-rate men gained and held power by running on the single issue that their opponents were Communists or were unwittingly doing the Communists' work. Nixon and his campaign manager, Murray Chotiner, seem to have been the first to use these tactics exclusively, but their success quickly attracted others, like George Smathers in Florida and, of course, Joseph McCarthy in Wisconsin. Smathers, in an especially crude anti-Communist campaign against the incumbent Senator Claude Pepper, ran "on the principle of the free state against the jail state." Pepper, he said, "is now on trial in Florida. Arrayed against him will be loyal Americans." On Pepper's side would be "all the socialists, all the radicals, and all the fellow travelers." In at least one speech, to what he considered an unsophisticated audience, he used the truth: "Are you aware that Claude Pepper is known all over Washington as a shameless extrovert? Not only that, but this man is reliably reported to practice nepotism with his sister-in-law, and he has a sister who was once a thespian. . . . Worst of all, it is an established fact that Mr. Pepper, before his marriage, practiced celibacy."

Nixon and Chotiner, however, were four years ahead of Smathers. In their successful 1946 Congressional election against the incumbent Jerry Voorhis, they ran the country's first unabashed single-issue, anti-Communist campaign. In Nixon's words, Voorhis was "a lip-service American" fronting for "un-American elements, wittingly or otherwise," who was "consistently voting the Moscow-PAC-Henry Wallace line in Congress." It did not matter that Voorhis was a staunch anti-Communist whom the PAC (Political Action Committee) specifically *refused* to endorse—Nixon continued to pound on this theme throughout the race. There were actually two PACs in California, both left wing and both vehemently opposed to Voorhis, but nobody except poor Voorhis seemed interested in the facts. Voorhis "was endorsed by the PAC and allied with the left-wing group which had taken over the Democratic Party in California," proclaimed Nixon. "A vote for Nixon is a vote against the Communist-dominated PAC with its gigantic slush fund," proclaimed the Nixon ads. In the final days anonymous phone calls were made throughout the district in which the caller would ask, "Did you know Jerry Voorhis was a Communist?" Nixon's managers denied responsibility for the calls, but at least one caller claimed to have worked out of Republican headquarters.

Nixon's successful 1950 Senate race against Representative Helen Gahagan Douglas was even more vicious than the Voorhis campaign. Again there was only one issue for Nixon: Was his opponent a Red? Douglas was labeled the pink lady, and "pink sheets" explaining her "Communist" connections were distributed by the thousands. She had, it seems, "generally been found voting in the House of Representatives with Vito Marcantonio" (the most extreme left-wing Congressman at the time). She was not just voting with him but was "found voting" with him, a much more serious matter. For example, they both were "found voting" for a bill to provide milk for the lunches of schoolchildren. (Indeed, if anyone had looked, Nixon himself could have been found voting with Marcantonio over 50 percent of the time.) There was, in fact, according to Nixon, a "Douglas–Marcantonio axis" in the Congress, "voting time after time against measures that are for the security of this country." To cap the campaign, Nixon brought McCarthy into California for one day to contribute his opinion that "The chips are down between the American people and the Administration Commicrat Party of betrayal."

Nixon won the election, but not without some cost to himself. In the heat of the campaign a small southern California newspaper, the *Independent Review*, gave him the label Tricky Dick Nixon, and it stuck. It was, as one writer said, "too appropriate to be ignored."

Nixon's first real crisis occurred in 1952, when he was running for vice president with General Eisenhower. The general was taking the high road, and Nixon characteristically was mining the old Communists-in-government theme for whatever nuggets he could find, when early in the campaign it came to light that Nixon was the beneficiary of a secret fund set up by a number of rich contributors. Its purpose, as one of the donors admitted, was for Nixon's private use "to do the kind of selling job we wanted." In typical Chotiner fashion, Nixon tried to brush off the issue, but its impact hit the Eisenhower entourage with devastating force and left the general "staggered and shaken."

It was clear from the reaction of Ike's group that Nixon had to explain himself—be "clean as a hound's tooth"—or be dropped from the ticket. Explaining that the "smear" on his record was coming from the "Communists and crooks" in the Truman administration, Nixon went over Ike's head by scheduling a nationwide television speech, known thereafter as "the Checkers speech," to explain the secret fund and ask the people if he should stay on the ticket. The gist of his defense was not to deny anything—all the secret fund charges seemed to be true—but to explain that the fund was used to pay expenses that legally could not be charged to the government. This was an incredible defense since it was surely illegal, but it seemed to work. "Not one cent of that money went for my personal use," he said, but in fact every penny had gone to his personal use, as he made clear in outlining what the uses were. He then mentioned his little dog, Checkers, which he said was another gift to the Nixon family, and "Regardless of what they say about it, we're gonna keep it." (They had not said *anything* about it.) The rest of the speech was an attack on his accusers, and the result of it all was that he was kept on the ticket. "You're my boy," Eisenhower told him two days later, and the secret fund controversy was over.

So was Nixon's career, or so it seemed, in 1962 when he lost the California gubernatorial race. Some people thought he wanted the governorship as a base for a 1964 presidential candidacy, but more likely he meant it when he pledged to serve out a full term if he won. (By then he was like the boy who cried wolf: Nobody believed him, even when he was truthful.) President Kennedy looked unbeatable at the time, and it was good politics to have an excuse not to run until 1968. Also the incumbent governor, Pat Brown, seemed extremely vulnerable in a race against an ex-vice president who had just missed being president by a whisker two years previously.

One of the low points of the governor's race was the use of an altered photograph by Nixon and his campaign manager, H. R. Haldeman, showing Brown genuflecting to a Laotian girl in an earlier charity drive

"Here he comes now"—from *Herblock: A Cartoonist's Life* (Times Books, 1998).

for refugees. Substituting Soviet Premier Khrushchev for the Laotian girl made the photograph more effective for Nixon's purpose. Haldeman defended their action when it was exposed by pointing out that it was, after all, "a picture of Brown."

The lowest point was Nixon and Haldeman's attempt to trick Democrats into voting Republican by the use of a fraudulent postcard "poll." They formed a "Committee for the Preservation of the Democratic party in California" as an instrument for mailing 500,000 postcards to conservative California Democrats, soliciting their opinion of the "capture" of the Democratic Party by left-wing elements. (In most of Nixon's campaigns there was a group of "Democrats for Nixon," or a Democrats-for-something-other-than-Democrats group. It was suggested that if Nixon had helped the Nazis there would doubtless have been a "Jews for Hitler" group in Germany in 1933.) The idea was to publicize the predictable results of the "poll" as the majority opinion of all California Democrats.

The cards began with "Dear Fellow Democrat," and it was made "perfectly clear" that "This is not a plea for any candidate." The "capture" of the Democratic Party by "this left-wing minority" was then described, and the reader was asked, "as a Democrat, what do you feel we can do?" An innocent suggestion was added: "We can take acceptable Republicans—if we can find any." The only Republican in the governor's race, of course, was Nixon.

The scheme was discovered when a Nixon volunteer worker, assuming the cards she was addressing actually came from the Democrats, took them to Democratic headquarters in San Francisco. A court order was obtained to stop further mailing of the postcards and to stop the proposed publication of the results. The Democrats accepted an out-of-court settlement after the election, but the presiding judge filed his final judgment, naming Nixon and Haldeman as having "approved the [postcard] plan and project" and agreeing that the Republicans "would finance the project." There is almost no doubt that the judge would have convicted Nixon and ended his career then and there had the case not been dropped.

Thanks in part to the aborting of the "postcard poll," Nixon was soundly defeated by Brown. He suddenly decided on the morning after the election to tell off the press for its years of malice toward him. "Now that all the members of the press are so delighted that I have lost, I'd like to make a statement of my own," he began, and he ended fifteen minutes later with, "You won't have Nixon to kick around anymore, because, gentlemen, this is my last press conference."

After Nixon's supposed political death, as it was proclaimed by commentator Howard K. Smith in a television documentary, the campaigns of 1964 and off-year 1966 went on with the usual venom and free-flowing bilge. Barry Goldwater, the 1964 Republican candidate buried by the Lyndon Johnson landslide, was greatly impressed with the job the Democratic public relations people did on him. "If I hadn't known Barry Goldwater personally," he said, "I would have voted against the son-of-a-bitch myself." Johnson harbored no such bitterness—at first. "I seldom think of politics more than eighteen hours a day," he said in his happier times. But as the Vietnam War dragged on, with its damage to his popularity ratings, he began to share Goldwater's feelings. "Cast your bread upon the waters," he advised a reporter, "and the sharks will get it." Despairing of trying to satisfy his many critics, he said, "I feel like a hound bitch in the country. If you run, they chew your tail off; if you stand still, they slip it to you." He ultimately confounded his tormentors by refusing to run for reelection.

In one of the greatest miracles of American politics, Nixon rose from the ashes of his "last press conference" to become his party's nominee in the 1968 presidential election. This he was able to do because of the leadership vacuum left by the Goldwater debacle and in spite of such protests as "He hath lain four years in his grave, wherefore he stinketh." His Democratic opponent was Vice President Hubert Humphrey, LBJ's handpicked choice and the logical nominee after the incredible assassination of Robert F. Kennedy during the primaries. Governor Spiro Agnew of Maryland was Nixon's running mate.

Humphrey's candidacy was destroyed before it began by the abuse he took from the antiwar demonstrators and by the violence they suffered from the police at the Democratic convention in Chicago. He was even vilified by Democratic liberals, his brethren in the party. Many of them helped Nixon, his Republican opponent, by spending the campaign "contemplating their own virtues." "Choose if you can," said the *New Republic*, a supposedly liberal magazine, professing to see no difference between Humphrey, the stalwart liberal champion for twenty years, and Nixon, his antithesis, who had once implied that Harry Truman was a traitor. A Humphrey aide, referring to the dissident liberals, said, "Nothing would bring the real peaceniks back to our side unless Hubert urinated on a portrait of Lyndon Johnson in Times Square before television—and then they'd say to him, 'Why didn't you do it before?'" In spite of his horrible start, Humphrey almost won the election, losing to Nixon by less than half a percentage point. "I could have beaten the Republicans any time,"

Humphrey said, "but it's difficult to take on the Republicans and fight a guerrilla war in your own party at the same time."

Nixon won the election by hiring ad men to package him and advertise him as they would any other marketable commodity. His managers' only problem was Nixon himself, whom people rejected "as a reflex." "He says such incredible pap," one ad man said, that any hopes for success required "creating an image without saying anything." He "will be elected on what he didn't say," the theme ran. "What he says is gobbledygook anyway, of course." Everything was carefully programmed and controlled, even to the "spontaneous" Nixon responses in his many television roundtable discussions and his closing telethon. In the latter event, Nixon had a set of answers on cards and his staff had the questions already written out. When a viewer called in with a question similar to theirs, the staff read their own question and attributed it to the caller. Nixon, of course, was ready with the answer. "This is the way they'll be elected forevermore," one Nixon ad man said, and he added with uncanny accuracy, "The next guys up will be performers."

For the most part the Nixon campaign was a smooth operation, but there were occasional disagreements among his managers, some of whom objected to the use of "every goddamned cliché in the book." But the prevailing view was that the dissenters were "asses" who "missed the whole point." The Nixon ads were "meant to be trite." They had to be, for their intended audience: "persons like Spiro Agnew who had never made an original observation in their life. . . . John Wayne may sound bad to the people in New York, but he sounds great to the schmucks we're trying to reach . . . the people down there along the Yahoo Belt."

The most remarkable feature of Nixon's 1968 victory was his ability to conduct the campaign without taking a stand on the burning issue of the day—the Vietnam War. He insisted from the beginning that he had a "secret plan" for ending the war but for security reasons he could not reveal it to the voters until they elected him. That he never had to reveal his plan—or discuss whether he ever had one—and still he won is a tribute to his managers' ability to isolate him from the press and the public while at the same time making it appear that his campaign was the most open in history.

The last crisis in Nixon's career, the Watergate scandal, was brought on in the 1972 campaign by the arrests of a number of Republican operatives caught in the act of bugging the Democratic party headquarters in the Watergate office-and-apartment complex. Attorney General John

Mitchell was first blamed, perhaps, as one observer suggested, on the theory that he "was the only politician in Washington ignorant enough to think there was something worth listening to at the Democratic National Committee." After his record landslide victory over George McGovern, however, Nixon himself was soon engulfed by the scandal. A Senate committee was formed to investigate the Watergate charges and consider the questions constantly put before it by Republican Senator Howard Baker: "What did the president know and when did he know it?"

During the course of the investigation, it was discovered that for three years Nixon secretly had taped all his conversations without any of his visitors' knowledge or consent. Thus the tapes could answer both of Senator Baker's questions, but in the name of national security Nixon felt it wise not to make them available. As the tapes were extracted a few at a time under court order, it was discovered that many previous Nixon statements were "inoperative" (not true) or "at variance with the facts" (lies), and that eighteen-and-one-half minutes of one of the most crucial tapes—the one recording Nixon's first conversation with Haldeman after the Watergate break-in—had been manually erased five to nine times. A "sinister force" was responsible for the gap in the tape, according to General Alexander Haig, a top Nixon assistant, but only Nixon, Haldeman, and one other aide had access to the tapes.

To add to Nixon's problems, the Watergate investigation also brought out a number of financial irregularities in his affairs. Questions were raised about government spending to improve his two homes and about the backdating of deeds involved in the donation of his vice presidential papers to the National Archives. In the fall of 1973, in a series of public appearances ironically dubbed Operation Candor, Nixon responded to questions about his finances and made the remarkable statement, "I am not a crook," a point that no other president has ever felt the need to make. He later bragged about his handling of his job in the midst of Watergate, saying, "the tougher it gets, the cooler I get." It was to get much worse.

In mid-1974 a House committee voted a bill of impeachment of Nixon. But Baker's questions were still unanswered, and Nixon's supporters in the House demanded to see the "smoking gun" evidence of guilt. The "smoking gun" was produced in the form of the June 23, 1972, tape with Haldeman's suggestion that Nixon tell the FBI "to stay the hell out of this," to which Nixon replied, "All right, fine." His most loyal supporter,

Congressman Charles Wiggins, asked sarcastically, "Does he have another Checkers speech in him?" and Senator Baker's questions were answered: What did the president know? Everything. When did he know it? From the beginning.

Shortly after the "smoking gun" appeared, Richard Nixon ended his presidency, as no man has ever done, with a letter to the secretary of state: "Dear Mr. Secretary: I hereby resign the Office of President of the United States. Sincerely, Richard Nixon."

As a footnote on Watergate, tapes more damaging than those that destroyed the Nixon presidency were released in 1992, revealing his

From *Herblock: A Cartoonist's Life* (Times Books, 1998).

directives to steal documents and, if necessary, "sneak in [to government offices] in the middle of the night." He also liked Haldeman's proposal to break up anti-Nixon demonstrations by using "Murderers. Guys that really, you know, that's what they really do . . . and, uh, and hope they really hurt 'em." Perhaps the worst of all were the tapes reportedly showing Nixon and aide Charles Colson plotting to break into the apartment of the would-be assassin Arthur Bremer, who had shot and paralyzed Alabama Governor George C. Wallace in the 1972 campaign. The scheme, hatched on the very day of the shooting, was to implicate McGovern by planting Democratic Party literature in Bremer's apartment. Unfortunately for Nixon, the FBI acted quickly to seal off the apartment, and Nixon's courier had to be called back.

Nixon's life may be summed up as Winston Churchill summed up that of Stanley Baldwin, the frequent prime minister of England: "He occasionally stumbles over the truth but he always hastily picks himself up as if nothing had happened." Harry Truman put it more directly over

"I have just discovered that according to a secret tape of June 23, 1972, I *am* a crook" (Bill Sanders, *Milwaukee Journal*).

twenty years before Watergate. "Nixon is a shifty-eyed, goddamn liar," he said, and to bring the voters up to date, he noted during the 1960 campaign that anyone who voted for Nixon "ought to go to hell." Many years later, the noted reporter and columnist Helen Thomas made a speech in Chambersberg, Pennsylvania, where a member of the audience asked her when she first knew that Nixon was lying. "Without a flicker of an eyelash," Helen said, "I promptly replied: In 1946." John Sirica, the judge in the Watergate trials and a Republican who had voted three times for Nixon, closed the chapter on Watergate with a wish shared by many of his fellow Americans. He said, "I hope no political party will ever stoop so low as to embrace the likes of Richard Nixon again." Nixon's epitaph could be his secretary Rosemary Woods's reply when asked for "some funny stories about Mr. Nixon."

"There *are* no funny stories about Mr. Nixon," she said.

"They called me 'Honest Abe.' What did they call you?" (Ray Osrin, *Cleveland Plain Dealer*).

14

Peanuts and Teflon

G erald Ford, some said, was Nixon's revenge on the American people. At the height of the Watergate controversy, which ultimately did Nixon in, Vice President Spiro Agnew was charged with being a "common thief," as the chief prosecutor put it, and he resigned under the pressure of otherwise going to jail. Nixon chose Ford to succeed Agnew, but sitting behind his desk in the Oval Office he asked Governor Nelson Rockefeller of New York, "Can you imagine Jerry Ford sitting in this chair?" Ford did have a reputation for not being the smartest person in Congress, thanks to the efforts of Lyndon Johnson, who accused him of playing football at Michigan too many times without his helmet. A more telling crack was Johnson's charge, euphemistically reworded by the press: "Jerry Ford is too dumb to chew gum and walk at the same time."

On Nixon's resignation in August 1974, Ford, of course, became president, and he chose Rockefeller to be his vice president. Thus Ford was the first president who was neither elected president nor vice president, and Rockefeller was the second unelected vice president, after Ford.

In the 1976 election between Ford and Democrat Jimmy Carter, an ex-governor of Georgia and a rank outsider, Ford seemed to give credence to the rumors about his intelligence by continually bumping his head when boarding the presidential helicopter, pronouncing "judgment" as *judge-a-ment*, toasting "President Anwar Sadat [of Egypt] and the people of Israel," and telling the voters of New Hampshire that "All Americans in all forty-eight, I mean forty-nine, states can learn from your example." In the middle of the next passage, he explained that he of course meant fifty states. His worst and most costly gaffe in the campaign was his observance, in a nationally televised debate with Carter, that "there is no Soviet domination of Eastern Europe, and there never will be under a Ford administration." To show that this was not a slip on his part, Ford repeated this statement to the press the next day. By then the White House press corps had dubbed him "President Turkey" and accused him of "trying to sew up the klutz vote." (Ford was ahead of his time. In 1976, of course, all of Eastern Europe was behind the iron curtain and controlled by the Soviets, but fifteen years later the iron curtain was gone.)

Actually Ford was a very amiable, athletic, and honest president with a below-average flair for campaigning. On one occasion, after one of his speeches, he said to a reporter, "Not worth a damn, was it?" Ford was not

The Ford-Carter Debates (Syracuse Herald-Journal/Tim Atseff).

devoid of wit either. When asked to comment on whether Ronald Reagan, in his seventies without a single gray hair, used hair coloring, he said, "No, it's just prematurely orange."

What undoubtedly cost Ford the 1976 election was not his campaigning but an act committed before the campaign began. It was the September 1974 beauty: "I, Gerald R. Ford, President of the United States . . . have granted . . . a full, free and absolute pardon unto Richard Nixon for all offenses against the United States which he, Richard Nixon, has committed or may have committed or taken part in." Ford's reasoning in granting the pardon was that with it, "our long national nightmare is over." At the time, however, many observers were unkind enough to suspect openly that Nixon had appointed Ford with the understanding that the pardon would be forthcoming. Still others said Ford genuinely liked Nixon and that Nixon reminded him of Lincoln. (This, as Lincoln might have said, reminds us of a story—a Morris Udall story—about a candidate who was forced to admit that his opponent reminded him of Lincoln. Yes, he added, "If you can imagine a short, fat, dishonest Lincoln.")

The pardon at once made Ford vulnerable, and he almost lost his party's nomination to Reagan, who contested it vigorously. Ford, "the man who pardoned Nixon," Reagan noted, also was presiding over "the diplomatic and military decline of the United States" and was covering up his incompetence by promising all things to all people. "If he comes here with the same list of goodies as he did in Florida," Reagan told a North Carolina crowd, "the band won't know whether to play 'Hail to the Chief' or 'Santa Claus Is Coming to Town.'" Ford, in turn, denounced Reagan as a warmonger who had advocated sending troops to Vietnam, Angola, Rhodesia, Cuba, and Panama. "Governor Ronald Reagan couldn't start a war," a Ford ad said, but "President Ronald Reagan could." Carter contributed his opinion that it was "an almost unbelievable spectacle," with the "President of the United States deeply concerned about an ex-movie actor, traveling all over the nation to get a handful of delegates." He probably found it more believable four years later when the same ex-movie actor ran against him—and this time succeeded.

Vice President Rockefeller also made the news. He had bowed out as a candidate for reelection as a sop to the conservatives in the party,

Rocky's Farewell Salute (United Press International Photo).

but some of the more ardent ones wanted a categorical statement that he wasn't interested in the presidency even if something happened to Ford. "What would I do? . . . Resign? . . . that is the whole point of having a vice president," replied Rocky. Later in Houston, Texas, at a private meeting of southern Republican state chairmen, he said, "You got me out, you sons of bitches, now get off your asses." Still later he capped his career in a way that must be the envy of most politicians, by giving a group of hecklers the finger, recorded by the cameras for posterity.

Meanwhile Carter, who was also the owner of a large peanut business in Plains, Georgia, was running as a "peanut-farmer Billy Graham," who wanted "a government that is as good, and honest, and decent, and

Lincoln, Ford as himself (considered damning enough), and Nixon as Edsel (V. Roshkov, *Windsor Star*).

truthful, and fair, and competent, and idealistic, and compassionate, and as filled with love as are the American people." His workers asked, "Why Not the Best?" while Carter himself was content to point out that while he would not talk about Ford's pardoning of Nixon—*and Ford had done this*—there was "almost complete continuity" in policy in the "Nixon-Ford administration." Was it fair to link Ford to a man who was "fairly unsavory?" asked a reporter, to whom Carter replied, "It's not my fault that Nixon is unsavory."

Not to be outdone by Ford's gaffes, Carter began a series of his own. The most notable, and the one that demolished his huge lead in the polls, was his incredible interview with *Playboy* magazine. "I've looked on a lot of women with lust. I've committed adultery in my heart many times," the Democratic candidate for president said, "and God forgives me for it." But he couldn't condemn a man who "leaves his wife and shacks up with somebody out of wedlock. Christ says, Don't consider yourself better than someone else because one guy screws a whole bunch

Charles Brooks 1976. Copyright by *The Birmingham News*, 2003. All rights reserved. Reprinted with permission.

of women while the other guy is loyal to his wife." The interview predictably caused an uproar, particularly among Carter's evangelical friends. Carter's own pastor lamented his choice of words, and a New York preacher, evidently inexperienced with sexual slang, thought it *was* acceptable to condemn a man for "shacking down" with another man's wife. (As author Barbara Holland later pointed out, lusting in your heart annoys the voters; a president "should either not lust, like Nixon, or do something about it, like Kennedy.")

Carter managed to hang on and win the election, but by an even smaller electoral margin than John Kennedy's in 1960. He enjoyed the usual "honeymoon" with Congress and the voters, beginning with his historic walk down Pennsylvania Avenue after the inauguration. But by 1980 the twin devils of inflation and the energy crisis of the late 1970s had taken their toll on his presidency. He took seriously his campaign claim of being an outsider and consequently had trouble dealing with the House and Senate. ("He couldn't get the Pledge of Allegiance through Congress," complained one veteran congressman.) He became the first elected incumbent to be seriously challenged for his party's renomination since William Howard Taft in 1912 and the first since Herbert Hoover in 1932 to be denied reelection by the voters. He was blamed for all the country's ills, and the prevailing sentiment seemed to be as bad as that expressed by a writer in 1892, who called then-President Benjamin Harrison "a purely intellectual being" with "no bowels," whose reelection would mean "four more years in a dripping cave." (People must not have liked Harrison's successor, Grover Cleveland, much more, for on the day his term ended, one said, "On this auspicious day the sky is blue, the birds sing, and joy is unconfined. It is the last day of the Cleveland administration.")

In 1980 there were for the first time fifty-one primaries and caucuses, and thus it could be said that the voters chose the candidates—Carter and his Republican challenger Ronald Reagan—as well as the winner. The exception perhaps was Representative John Anderson, a third candidate, who was not chosen by anyone unless it was Reagan. As it turned out, Anderson helped Reagan by splitting the moderate vote in the Republican primaries and by providing the Democratic liberals with a safe place to deposit their votes in the general election.

Although the voters had picked the candidates, they quickly repented and adopted a "plague on both your houses" attitude toward Carter and Reagan. "May the worst man lose" seemed to be the popular view, and the slogan of Richard Tuck, the political prankster, was "Nixon in '80—Why not the worst?" The campaign was so dull that a *Newsweek* article trying to interest its readers in "the joy of non sex," seemed as exciting as the choices for president.

There was indeed very little humor in the campaign. Reagan got off one recorded joke when he pointed out that the third-century Roman emperor Diocletian had tried price controls and that they hadn't worked then either. "And I'm the only one here old enough to remember that," he added. His other jokes were unintentional, as when he indicted the redwood trees for producing more pollution than automobiles (prompt-

The 1980 choices (Steve Sack, reprinted with permission from the *Minneapolis Star and Tribune*).

ing California students to put signs on the venerable trees: "Stop me before I kill again."), and when he cited the requirements of drivers' licenses as evidence of our loss of freedom under the Democrats. He refrained from cracking jokes perhaps because he didn't want to add to his reputation as a glib actor whose candidacy itself was a joke. Carter, on the other hand, was as evangelical as he was in 1976. He did provide one chuckle, however, in his acceptance speech, when he referred to Hubert Humphrey as that great American senator "Hubert Horatio Hornblower."

Part of Carter's grim task was to keep the public from knowing of Anderson's candidacy, whose appeal was to Carter's natural constituency rather than Reagan's. This job was made more difficult daily as the newscasters kept referring to Carter, Reagan, and Anderson as the "three major candidates." The *New Republic* editorialized that "Anderson can win," when everyone else thought—rightly—that he would not get a single electoral vote. The League of Women Voters added to Carter's agony by inviting the "three major candidates" to engage in a debate. The League, whom in his earlier days Reagan had referred to as a bunch of "Rhine Maidens," issued their invitation just after the Democratic convention ended, when the momentum was clearly with Carter, and he had seemed to close the awesome gap in the polls. A three-way debate giving Anderson credence as a major candidate would have been suicidal, and thus Carter wisely declined the offer. The "debate" was held anyway between Reagan and Anderson, and Carter's bandwagon never got back on track.

Carter's biggest problem, however, was one that was totally out of his control. Iranian fanatics, with the blessing of the Ayatollah Khomeini's government, seized the American embassy in Tehran and held the American diplomats hostage until after the election. Indeed, as Carter's luck had it, the election occurred on the one-year anniversary of the taking of the hostages, so it was hard for the voters not to be aware of the problem. An unsuccessful rescue attempt was made, but the Carter luck held, as one helicopter malfunctioned and another collided with a plane in the Iranian desert, forcing the abortion of the mission.

The final irony of the campaign came in the last week, when Carter did agree to debate. Carter looked "presidential" and highly knowledgeable, but the result was a disaster for him. The polls immediately following the debate showed the contest going from a horse race to a Reagan electoral landslide. Carter, an honest and highly intelligent man,

Reagan's and Carter's views of each other (*Syracuse Herald-Journal*/Tim Atseff).

The public's view of the candidates (*Syracuse Herald-Journal*/Tim Atseff).

had worked hard to be a good president, but the times were difficult, and the voters yearned for a change. They seemed, however, reluctant to vote for Reagan because he seemed to be a trigger-happy extremist. This perception changed during the debate, when he came across as an amiable, reasonable candidate. A prime example was when a smiling Reagan replied to a point made by Carter with "There you go again, Mr. President." (Reagan's good showing might also be attributed to the fact, which surfaced in 1983, that his side had unethically obtained—not to say stolen—a copy of Carter's briefing notebook for the debate.)

For the most part, Reagan's presidency was a love affair with the American people. After a rocky start, the economy improved and the horrendous double-digit inflation was brought under control by the Federal Reserve's incredibly tight money policy. The former actor's mastery of the

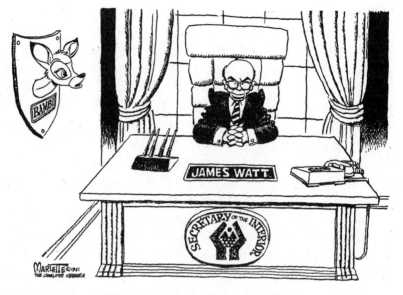

(*The Charlotte Observer*/Doug Marlette)

television medium earned him the nickname the Great Communicator. Even things that went wrong were not held against him. U.S. Marines he'd stationed in Lebanon were slaughtered by fanatics, the national debt tripled during his presidency, and his secretary of the interior, James Watt, seemed bent on destroying the nation's natural resources. (Humorist Art Buchwald said Watt was asked the old question, Does a tree falling in the forest make a noise if nobody is there to hear it? His answer was, "What is a tree doing in the forest in the first place?") And his Environmental Protection Agency head, Ann Burford, did little to protect the environment. But none of this stuck to Ronald Reagan, prompting Congresswoman Pat Schroeder to label him "the Teflon president."

The Teflon was strongly in place during the 1984 election, as Reagan and his vice president, George Bush, campaigned for reelection against Walter Mondale, Carter's vice president, and New York Representative Geraldine Ferraro, the first woman in American history to be nominated on a major party ticket. She also very nearly became the first vice presidential candidate to be called a bitch, when Bush's wife, Barbara, said Ferraro was "a four million dollar—I can't say it, but it rhymes with 'rich.'"

Reagan began the campaign some eighteen points ahead in the polls and ended up winning by about the same margin. The election, therefore, could have been dispensed with, for all the good it did. This was true also for all the jokes it generated. Reagan seemed to have three. He said at one point he was about to tell Mondale he was "taxing my patience," but decided against it, since "that's the only tax he hasn't thought about." When a newsman asked what could be done about the annual huge deficit, Reagan answered, "the deficit is big enough to take care of itself." The Gipper (another Reagan nickname, dating back to his movie role of Notre Dame's football hero George Gipp) also took a live radio microphone, thinking it was off, and said, "My fellow Americans, I'm pleased to tell you today that I've signed legislation that would outlaw Russia forever. We begin bombing in five minutes." Mondale said he "assumed it was a joke."

On the Democratic side, Senator Gary Hart almost stopped the Mondale drive for the nomination by winning a number of early primaries. Hart campaigned on his "New Ideas" platform, and when it developed that Hart had previously shortened his name from Hartpence and inexplicably had listed his birth year as 1937 instead of 1936, newsman John Chancellor said that Hart did indeed have two new ideas: his name and his age. Hart's campaign collapsed, however, in the face of the Wendy's hamburger ad, "Where's the beef?" which Mondale used constantly to question the substance of Hart's program. Later in the general election, comedian Mark Russell said that, to liven things up, Mondale called Wendy's to see if they had any new slogans.

The election also had its oddities. Republican Reagan swiped the mantle of Democrats Franklin D. Roosevelt and John F. Kennedy, praising them at every opportunity. At one point he actually used Harry Truman's 1948 whistlestop train on a campaign trip. Meanwhile Mondale postured against the unbalanced Reagan budgets like an old-line Republican. He even promised to raise taxes if elected, a very strange campaign tactic, but the voters preferred Reagan's alternative of borrowing $200 billion per year. In another odd twist of 1984, the Chicago Cubs, everybody's favorite also-ran, actually won the National League East pennant. They of course lost the post-season playoffs.

Connoisseurs also noted some vitriol in the campaign other than Mrs. Bush's. Vice President Bush was called Reagan's cheerleader and Reagan's lapdog, and cartoonist Garry Trudeau, in his comic strip *Doonesbury*, accused Bush of placing his manhood in a blind trust. As for Reagan, House Speaker Tip O'Neill said it was "sinful that he is president of the United States," because "he only works three to three and a half hours a day" and was "ignorant of every sphere of knowledge." (O'Neill thus went along with the wishes of Reagan's 1980 campaign manager, John Sears, who had said, "We'd rather have you say he's too ignorant than too old.") Reagan pounded Mondale with the Carter-Mondale connection, and his aides advised, "Don't let the public forget that Mondale's first name is Carter."

The vice presidential candidates also debated. Bush seemed to condescend to Ferraro, which seemed to irritate her, but undoubtedly the most irritating thing from her point of view was his statement after the debate that "I kicked a little ass."

The age issue also surfaced. (After all, Reagan *was* two years older than Arizona, as humorist Lewis Grizzard pointed out later.) In the first Reagan-Mondale debate, Mondale looked like the president of the United States, and the Great Communicator looked as if he were at sea. His stumbling and hesitation on the air and his astonishingly weak summation took everybody by surprise, and one reporter wondered if he was playing with a "full-deck." The *Wall Street Journal*, supposedly friendly to him, asked in the front-page headline, "Is Oldest U.S. President Now Showing His Age?" Fortunately for Reagan, his Teflon was intact, and the age issue caused only a slight ripple in the polls. In the second debate, Reagan regained the initiative by solemnly declaring that he would "not take advantage of my opponent's youth and inexperience" by exploiting his age. Reagan won in a landslide, with Mondale carrying only his home state of Minnesota and the District of Columbia.

An unwritten rule in American politics seems to be that winners of landslide victories pay dearly for them. After Franklin D. Roosevelt's great victory in 1936, he got himself into big trouble with the voters with his 1937 Supreme Court packing plan. After Lyndon Johnson's 1964 landslide victory, he was hounded from office, deciding not to run for reelection. And, of course, Richard Nixon's huge 1972 win was followed by his resignation as president. The tradition was continued with Ronald Reagan. His 1984 landslide election seemed to be an exception, until late 1986 when gaping holes were torn in the Teflon presidency by yet another Iranian fiasco.

At that time, it developed that Reagan, despite a vow never to deal with terrorists, had secretly shipped arms through the Israelis to the Iranians in return for their help in securing the release of still more American hostages held in Lebanon. It also came out that a team operating in the White House basement had illegally diverted the Iranian arms money to the Nicaraguan Contras, a group carrying on a guerrilla war with the Nicaraguan leftist government. In a TV appearance, Reagan first said he approved the arms deal in advance, the entire arms shipment "could be put in one cargo plane, and there would be plenty of room left over," and no third country was involved. His aides had repudiated all these positions earlier, and then explained that the president didn't know what he was talking about. Reagan later said he didn't approve the arms

Reagan fingering Carter for all the ills of the 1980s (*Tribune Media Services*/Jack Ohman, copyright © 1984. Reprinted by permission).

deal in advance, but did it after the fact. Finally, he said, "The simple truth is, I don't remember." Reagan's press secretary didn't help matters when, in a slip of the tongue, he promised the White House press corps to "find out who is president."

Cartoons began appearing showing Reagan in a dunce cap and as a trophy along with Carter on the Ayatollah Khomeini's mantelpiece, and his popularity rating dropped to 37 percent. Truman's former secretary of defense, Clark Clifford, called him "an amiable dunce," and wags began asking, in Watergate fashion, "What did the president forget, and when did he forget it?" When the Great Communicator looked the American people in the eye on television and said, "We did not trade arms for hostages," did he lie, or did he forget? Did he illegally divert money to the Contras, or did he really not know what was going on in his own administration? In the latter case, as one observer put it, his defense was "We're not crooked. We're stupid." The Democrats also had a dilemma, according to House Speaker Jim Wright, who said, "For six years we went around saying Ronald Reagan didn't know what was going on. And now when he says the same thing about himself, we say he's lying."

The Iran-Contra charges, if true, were more impeachable than any of the Watergate charges leveled against Nixon. More treasonable even

HE WAS THE ONLY JUROR WE COULD FIND WHO KNEW ABSOLUTELY NOTHING ABOUT THE IRAN—CONTRA AFFAIR .....

Reagan as juror in the Iran-Contra trial of his aide Oliver North (Mike Peters © Grimmy Inc. Distributed by King Features Syndicate).

Nixon vs. Reagan (*Seattle Post Intelligencer* 1987/Steve Greenberg, reprinted with permission).

(©1985, John Trever, *Albuquerque Journal*. Reprinted by permission.)

than Iran-Contra was the "October Surprise" charge in the late 1980s that Reagan and members of his 1980 campaign team, notably William Casey, conspired with the Iranians to keep the American hostages until after the election. Their theory went that otherwise Carter would, in an October surprise, announce the release of the hostages and win the election. The evidence was circumstantial: In a very odd coincidence, the hostages were released immediately upon Reagan's taking the oath of office, Casey *was* a cloak-and-dagger type who worked in intelligence with the government during World War II and who headed the CIA under Reagan, his whereabouts could not be accounted for during the alleged meetings in Europe with the Iranians, and arms *were* shipped secretly to Iran through Israel, beginning almost immediately after Reagan took office. A number of eyewitnesses placed Casey at the meetings, but they were considered unreliable.

Casey died just before these scandals broke, and no "smoking gun" could be found. A congressional committee held public hearings on Iran-Contra, but no administration officials higher than the chairman of the National Security Council were charged. The public, therefore, was left to wonder if the charges were true or if they were ridiculous.

The jury will be out for some time on President Reagan because eventually the records of that era will be made public. His Teflon may hold and, as his admirers insist, he may be rated as one of the best presidents of the twentieth century. He was, after all, the first since Dwight D. Eisenhower to serve two terms and enjoy tremendous popularity. On the other hand, as one detractor suggested, his memorial could be a gaping hole in the ground in the shape of an inverted Washington Monument symbolizing all his deficits.

15

Read My Lips

I n 1988 the most popular television program was *The Cosby Show*; the Baltimore Orioles set a major league record by losing their first twenty-one games of the season; televangelist Jimmy Swaggart, in a tearful on-the-air performance, confessed to an unspecified sin (which we can now specify: a tryst with a New Orleans whore); Winning Colors became only the third filly ever to win the Kentucky Derby; Steffi Graf became only the fifth player to win tennis's Grand Slam; and the best-selling books were Tom Clancy's *The Cardinal of the Kremlin* and Tom Wolfe's *The Bonfire of the Vanities.* The new abortion pill RU486, said to be "safer and less expensive than surgery," was introduced in Paris; Irving Berlin turned 100; and the Shroud of Turin, revered by many as the cloth that covered the body of Jesus after His crucifixion, was found to date only from the thirteenth century. It was also a year in which we were treated to a "trivial pursuit of the presidency" in an election called by authors Jack Germond and Jules Witcover "perhaps the most mean-spirited and negative campaign in modern-day American political history." Thus it could be said that in 1988 we came full circle from 1828 and 1840, where we began our narrative.

The 1988 election was only the second since 1960 when neither candidate was an incumbent seeking reelection. Also, as in 1960, one of the candidates was the vice president in a highly popular administration, and the other was a challenger from Massachusetts. But this time the results were reversed, with the promotion to the presidency of the first sitting vice president since Martin Van Buren in 1836. To many, however, the 1988 election invited more comparison with 1840 than with 1960. In 1840 Van Buren was defeated for a second term by General William Henry Harrison, who trivialized the issues in a highly negative campaign, noted as the "jolliest and most idiotic in our history." After the 1840 campaign, as we noted earlier, a newspaper editor expressed hope that "No more may the world see coons, cabins, and cider usurp the place of principles, nor doggerel verse elicit a shout, while argument, principle, and reason are passed by with a derisive sneer." A post-1988 election letter to the editor of *Newsweek*, similar in tone, expressed the hope that "we realize that decisions like [those the voters made in the campaign] are costly for our future—and think twice when the next flag-waving, anthem-humming politician tries to obscure the issues and misuse the media."

Vice President George Bush was the Republican candidate with the advantage of incumbency, but he won the nomination only after a spirited fight in the primaries. President Reagan, of course, was constitutionally limited to two terms and could not run again, though comedian Jay Leno said he was going to try. "They've added up his vacations and nap times," said Leno, "and are claiming he's only served half a term."

Bush's principal opponent in the primaries was Senator Bob Dole, the minority leader and perhaps the Senate wit. (A sample of the Dole wit was his reference to Presidents Carter, Ford, and Nixon, in that order, as "See no evil, hear no evil, and evil.") In the New Hampshire primary, Bush defeated Dole with his "straddle ad," in which he accused the senator of "straddling" the issue of taxes. Dole was not amused and, before bowing out, called on Bush to "stop lying about my record." He also told a supporter of another candidate, Representative Jack Kemp, to "get back in your cave."

An irony, however, was that Dole helped Bush on the Iran-Contra affair, which was still a hot issue because Bush was widely perceived to be lying about his role in it. He claimed to be "out of the loop" when the arms-for-hostages deal was made but was running as Reagan's vice president who had helped shape the world of the 1980s. Many considered Dole the only candidate with the stature and insider knowledge to go up against Bush on Iran-Contra, and when his candidacy collapsed the issue faded with it. Lee Atwater, Bush's campaign manager, thus could say that Iran-Contra "was a royal pain in the ass, but it finished off Dole." Bush got rid of still another rival, Governor Pierre "Pete" DuPont of Delaware, by publicly calling him Pierre. This was Atwater's method of changing folksy Pete to one of the wealthy DuPonts.

The Reverend Pat Robertson, a TV evangelist, became a candidate, he said, because of pressure from God. The Almighty also tacked on a proviso: At least three million earthly souls would have to indicate their support in writing, and presumably with their money as well. Robertson's timing was bad, however, because of the recent decline in popularity of such televangelists as Swaggart, whose troubles have already been noted, and Oral Roberts, who announced that God would kill him unless viewers sent in $8 million almost immediately. (Unfortunately, viewers were not able to see if the Lord would really carry out the threat because someone *did* send in the money.) Also, Jim Bakker, the TV preacher of PTL (Praise the Lord), confessed he wasn't using his huge contributions exclusively to feed the hungry and clothe the naked (particularly the latter, in the case of the church secretary he bedded down with and to whom he was paying blackmail). A Bakker associate had urged that PTL be saved by its supporters' getting out their checkbooks, but wags used the occasion to change PTL to "Pay The Lady" and "Pass The Loot," and humorist Lewis Grizzard said it "was down the toilet, where it belonged."

With all the other candidates "finished off," Bush had easy sailing in the remaining primaries, notably the South Carolina primary and the so-called Super Tuesday primaries in March. Also, Reagan finally endorsed Bush, or so it seemed. No one could be certain, since in his endorsement he pronounced *Bush* to rhyme with *brush*. (First Lady Nancy Reagan supposedly had another name, "Whiney," for the vice president, who had gained her enmity in the 1980 primaries when he dubbed Reagan's economic program "voodoo economics.")

With Reagan barred from reelection, the Democrats sensed a chance to win, and a multitude of them entered the primaries. At the start Gary Hart of 1984 fame was the frontrunner. Hart soon proved the pundits right who thought Democrats didn't know how to win. (Their idea of assembling a firing squad, one said, is to form a circle.) He replied to rumors of his womanizing by issuing a challenge: "Put a tail on me . . . you'll be very bored." A *Miami Herald* reporter did just that and printed a Sunday edition story alleging that Hart "had spent Friday night and most of Saturday in his Capitol Hill town house with a young woman" (later identified as Miami model Donna Rice). The story simmered for a month and ended with Hart's withdrawal from the race and the publication in a gossip newspaper of a picture of Rice sitting on Hart's lap on a pier next to their rented yacht, *Monkey Business*. Hart perhaps could take some comfort in Richard Nixon's statement that he was proud of him, and from columnist Donald Kaul's reassuring question, "Hey! Would Richard Nixon lie?" Kaul also noted sympathetically that "We've already had a president who confessed to lusting in his heart; the only difference with Hart is that he has a better sense of anatomy."

Former Governor Bruce Babbitt, of Arizona, provided one of the more memorable lines from the primary campaign when he said that "George Bush reminds every woman of her first husband," a remark attributed also to humorist Art Buchwald. Representative Morris Udall, who wasn't running, contributed his opinion that "Reaganomics was

" THE WHITE HOUSE? YOU CAN'T GET THERE FROM HERE!"

Hart's candidacy wrecked by "Monkey Business" (*The Atlanta Constitution*/Doug Marlette).

based on the principle that the rich and poor will get the same amount of ice, but the poor will get theirs in winter." (Observations like this probably prompted the short note Udall said he got from a constituent: "You are a no good son of a bitch. Suggest you resign. Strong letter follows.") Another candidate of note was former Senator Paul Tsongas, who urged the Democrats to "try winning and see what it feels like. If we don't like it, we can go back to our traditions."

Jesse Jackson, another 1984 holdover, and Governor Michael Dukakis of Massachusetts emerged from the final group of seven Democrats, inevitably termed "the seven dwarfs," as the two finalists. Dukakis was the frontrunner and eventually won, but Jackson—who had no chance because the country was not ready for a black president—also had nothing to lose by continuing to run. When the primaries were over, Jackson thought he had enough delegates to be considered for the vice presidency, but Dukakis chose Senator Lloyd Bentsen of Texas, thus repeating the Massachusetts-Texas alliance that John Kennedy had forged in 1960.

The Democratic convention was held first, and speaker after speaker derided Bush. The keynoter, Ann Richards of Texas, ridiculed him as a counterfeit Texan who was "born with a silver foot in his mouth." (Bush, who owned a mansion in Maine, claimed Texas as his home state, but his "home" was reported to be a suite in a Houston hotel, which later declared bankruptcy.) Senator Ted Kennedy ticked off a list of supposed Reagan failures and asked after each item, "Where was George?" And in an interview with an Atlanta newspaper, Jimmy Carter noted that Bush has a "very serious problem of silliness." Watching the convention on television, Roger Ailes, Bush's media expert, decided, "Oh, boy, we got trouble here." The polls confirmed Ailes's worries, with one showing Dukakis with a postconvention seventeen-point lead.

Between the conventions, Atwater and Bush began trying out material Atwater had collected in April, the "stuff," Atwater said, "to beat this little bastard [Dukakis] with." These were the "issues" of the Massachusetts prison furlough program, Dukakis's veto of a Pledge of Allegiance bill, and the pollution of Boston Harbor. These were bogus issues in a presidential campaign, but even so, Dukakis seemed to be on the right side of all of them. The furlough program was a modern penal tool, similar to those commonly used in most states; the pledge bill was designed to *force* teachers to lead the Pledge of Allegiance to the flag, which seems un-American on its face; and Boston Harbor's condition more accurately could be blamed on Reagan's Environmental Protection Agency than on the local government. But because a convicted murderer named Willie Horton, released for a weekend, had fled and committed rape, Bush was able to use the furlough program to make Dukakis seem soft on crime. The pledge veto, of course, was used to make him seem soft on patriotism. Also, since Horton was black, a fact made clear by the ads, Bush was able to exploit white fears of black criminals without openly appearing to be a racist.

Another setback for Dukakis was a rumor that he was mentally ill, put out by supporters of perennial fringe candidate Lyndon LaRouche, who had also charged Queen Elizabeth II with being a dope pusher. This farcical assertion would have had little or no impact except for a Reagan wisecrack made to the press ten days after the convention. Asked whether Dukakis should release his medical records, Reagan said, "I'm not going to pick on an invalid." He later said, "I think I was kidding, but I don't think I should have said what I said." Dukakis's lead, nevertheless, fell eight points, which were never regained.

When the Republican convention began, the polls showed the race dead even, but the pundits still insisted Bush's acceptance speech had to be "the speech of his life." He also had to pick a vice presidential running mate. ("Bush and Bush," was New York Governor Mario Cuomo's pick as the weakest GOP ticket.) After promising "a fantastic choice," Bush dismayed many of his friends and caused an uproar in the press by selecting Senator Dan Quayle of Indiana. (Particularly disappointed, one supposes, were the wags who wanted Jeane Kirkpatrick, former ambassador to the U.N., because, "She'd add some macho to the ticket.") Quayle was young and thought by many to be a lightweight, but most importantly he had evaded the draft during the Vietnam War. This wasn't so bad in itself—millions of other young men opposed to the war dodged the draft—but Quayle was a hawk (some said a "chicken hawk") who built his career by supporting the war. As writer Studs Terkel noted, "It's not just evading the draft, but it's Rambo evading the draft." In defending himself, Quayle said, "I did not know in 1969 that I would be in this room today [running for vice president]." Bush noted that Quayle "did not burn his draft card [nor the American flag]."

The convention proceeded in spite of the Quayle flap, and Bush, some said, did give the speech of his life. He promised a "kinder and gentler nation" (interpreted by some as a slap at outgoing president Reagan), promised 30 million new jobs, and pledged not to raise taxes. Reagan had earlier used a Clint Eastwood movie line, "Make my day," if Congress threatened to raise taxes, and Bush used a similar, Eastwood-like line in making his promise. "Read my lips," he said. "No new taxes!" (Humorist Mark Russell, however, was not fooled. "Read *my* lips," he said. "They're going to raise the old ones.")

Bush came out of the convention transformed from a "wimpish Casper Milquetoast into Jack the Ripper." He and Atwater concentrated on Atwater's "issues": Willie Horton, the Pledge of Allegiance, Boston Harbor, and for good measure, the American Civil Liberties Union, of which Dukakis was a "proud member." As one observer noted, these topics had no relevance, but they provided excellent videotape. "We gave them soundbites," Ailes said, in explaining why the television medium cooperated to get the Bush attacks on the air. In every edition of the evening news, Bush questioned Dukakis's patriotism ("What *is* his problem with the Pledge?"), his devotion to the environment ("He wants to do for the nation what he's done for Boston Harbor"), or his judgment (he was "opposed to every new weapons system since the slingshot" and, even worse, was "a card-carrying member of the ACLU"). And, of course, in every speech was "Read my lips. No new taxes."

Bush also kept Atwater's promise to "make Willie Horton a household word," with the "revolving door" ad, showing a line of prisoners being furloughed, presumably to rape and pillage. Pictures of Horton and Dukakis were shown together with the caption, "Is this your pro-family team?" Republican Senator Steve Symms got into the act by accusing Dukakis's wife Kitty of burning the flag. The attacks were so relentless and so effective that Atwater said he actually "felt sorry" for Dukakis. Bush himself became uncomfortable, lamenting toward the end what he had to do to win. "I want to get back on the issues," he said to Ailes, "and quit talking about *him*." "We plan to do that November 9th [the day after the election]," Ailes replied. Jim Baker, Bush's campaign director, justified the negative ads. "They were the only way we could assure Dukakis's defeat," he said.

Finally the networks rebelled when Bush visited a flag factory in New Jersey where he stated that "flag sales are doing well and America is doing

Bush, the former "wimp," celebrates his Super Tuesday victory (*Atlanta Constitution*/Doug Marlette).

well." All the networks juxtaposed that scene with an earlier one, in which Bush had been nonplussed about the number of Americans without health insurance as well as what to do about it. They showed Dukakis asking derisively, "Where is George Bush? He's visiting a flag factory. George, don't you think it's about time you came out from behind the flag and told us what you intend to do to provide basic health insurance for 37 million Americans?" It was "a flag too far," conceded Ailes.

More puzzling than Bush's getting away with his slash-and-burn methods, for which he paid no penalty and suffered no reprisals, was Dukakis's refusal to fight back. "He just didn't get it," Atwater said. One of Dukakis's advertising men, Ed McCabe, was more direct: "There's one thing the American people dislike more than someone who fights dirty. That's someone who climbs into the ring and won't fight. That's what really happened here. He threw the fight."

There were two presidential debates and a vice presidential debate. The first presidential debate, the polls showed, was a slight victory for Dukakis, though Bush held on to a six-point lead gained since the GOP convention. In the debate Dukakis seemed cold and humorless and Bush, at times, was incoherent. It showed the voters, columnist Mary McGrory said, "caught between a chilly governor . . . and a clumsy vice president.

[Reagan] was an idolized fact-mangler," as shown by his statement at the GOP convention that "Facts are stupid things," when he meant to quote John Adams's dictum, "Facts are stubborn things." But Bush, she added, "massacred facts like a mad killer in a mall." (Throughout the campaign he *did* say startling things like, "We [he and Reagan] have had sex," when he meant to say "had setbacks," "I stand for antibigotry, anti-Semitism . . ." and, in a prepared speech to the American Legion, "This [September 7] is Pearl Harbor Day . . ." Things got so bad that the *New Republic* wondered in an editorial if Bush was aphasic.)

Columnist David Sarasohn said the debate "displayed two of the most frightening things seen on television since the adoption of the Broadcasters Code: Michael Dukakis trying to smile and George Bush trying to think. Dukakis's smile looks like someone told to open wide for root canal work, and his wit may make Democrats yearn for the rollicking days of Walter Mondale . . ." (Dukakis did have wit, however, though he didn't show it until two years after the debates. "What do you do," he asked, "if you're in the room with Muammar Qaddafi, Saddam Hussein, and John Sununu [his nemesis in the 1988 campaign] and you have a gun that has only two bullets?" Answer: "Shoot Sununu twice.")

The highlight of the vice presidential debate was an exchange between Bentsen and Quayle over Quayle's experience. In answer to a panelist's question, Quayle said, "I have as much experience in the Congress as Jack Kennedy had when he sought the presidency." At this point Bentsen, who apparently had been waiting for this chance, glared at Quayle and retorted, "Senator, I served with Jack Kennedy. I knew Jack Kennedy. Jack Kennedy was a friend of mine. Senator, you're no Jack Kennedy." Bentsen, of course, won the debate—some polls said four to one—and the "Kennedy thing" dogged Quayle for weeks. ("What did Marilyn Quayle [his wife] say to Dan Quayle after making love?" ran one joke. Answer: "Senator, you're no Jack Kennedy.") Curiously, the debate gained Dukakis little ground on Bush, who still led by some six points.

The last presidential debate opened with CNN anchorman Bernard Shaw asking the governor if he would favor the death penalty for the killer if "Kitty Dukakis were raped and murdered." Dukakis might have turned the election around if he had replied that it wouldn't be necessary—he would kill the perpetrator himself, but instead he launched into a scholarly discussion of the death penalty and why he opposed it. He showed as

Lincoln-Douglas horrified by Bush-Dukakis debates (Scott Stantis, ©1988, *The Commercial Appeal*, Memphis, Tenn.).

much emotion, an observer said, as he might have about an offender caught "jaywalking." "I blew it," Dukakis said later, and writer Barbara Ehrenreich said that "since [Dukakis] was pro-rape," it wasn't easy to explain the gender gap (Dukakis's margin over Bush among women).

Throughout the campaign Bush had constantly labeled Dukakis a liberal, in a manner suggesting that "liberal" was another word for "leper." Dukakis had obliged by running from the "L word" as if it *were* leprous. At the end he decided to be himself and proclaimed that he was indeed a liberal—"a liberal in the tradition of Franklin Roosevelt and Harry Truman and John Kennedy." This seemed to help him somewhat in the polls (there was even talk of a "Dukakis surge"), but he soon dropped the subject when Bush gleefully said, I told you so.

The race did tighten somewhat, and the final count was closer than the last published polls, with Bush winning by 53.9 percent of the popular vote and 426 electoral votes. Dukakis had 46.1 percent and 112 electoral votes, both much better showings than Mondale's in 1984. Dukakis, like Thomas E. Dewey in 1948, was a competent man who lost because he underestimated and failed to respond to his opponent's campaign tactics. As for Bush, he won, Donald Kaul said, with a mandate to "lead the nation in the Pledge of Allegiance."

It's the Economy, Stupid

George Bush was the first sitting vice president since Martin Van Buren to be elected president. And, like Van Buren in 1840, Bush became a one-term president in 1992, when Arkansas Governor Bill Clinton and his running mate, Senator Al Gore, defeated the Bush-Quayle ticket. It was an odd campaign, in which Texas billionaire Ross Perot got the most popular votes of any third-party candidate since Theodore Roosevelt in 1912, and the Apathy Party candidate promised, if elected, not to steal for the first two years. Clinton thus became the first president born after World War II and the first sitting governor to win the White House since Franklin D. Roosevelt in 1932. And Clinton and Gore, of course, were also the first baby boomers to be elected to the nation's two highest offices. All three candidates, Bush, Clinton, and Gore, were left-handed, another oddity, considering that before Bush we'd had only three left-handed presidents: Garfield, Truman, and Ford.

The biggest oddity of the campaign was undoubtedly Bush's roller coaster ride in the polls. Early in his term he broke his solemn pledge of "Read my lips. No new taxes," eliciting cries from the voters of "Read our lips. No second term!" Even one of the characters in the comic strip

Bush campaign on trust (Henry Payne. Reprinted by permission of United Feature Syndicate, Inc.).

B.C. got into the act, saying "Show me a politician that only speaks half-truths and I'll show you a guy that says 'Read my lip.'"

Bush also became the first president to lead an assault on the Bill of Rights, when he tried unsuccessfully to pass an anti-flag-burning amendment to the Constitution, which would have violated the first Amendment. (Jay Leno said he understood Bush's zeal: "If you wrapped yourself in the flag like he does, you wouldn't want anybody setting fire to it.")

These affronts to the voters, however, were forgotten midway through his term, when he skillfully forged a U.N. coalition of forces that drove Iraqi dictator Saddam Hussein out of Kuwait in the Persian Gulf War. Bush's polls peaked at 91 percent, and none of the big-name Democrats could be lured into running against him. The economy, however, went into recession, and by the time of the election his popularity was at 30 percent, and Bush T-shirts began appearing with the caption "Read my lips: No more jobs."

Bush's popularity was so low that when he went on the field of baseball's All Star game in July with baseball great Ted Williams, the crowd booed. Bush said he detected no animosity, prompting some wit to note that the crowd was booing Williams!

Bush tried hard to divert voters from the economy, with charges that Democrats were "cultural elitists," "bozos," and "tree-hugging environmentalists," or "ozone men," who had no "family values" and very little religion. (They "did not have the three letters *G-O-D* in their party platform," Bush noted.) Clinton, he said, was the failed governor of a small state "located somewhere between Texas and Oklahoma" [which, wags noted, made it an island in the Red River]. Republican Senator Jake Garn called "Bill Clinton and Al Gore . . . a team of pretty boys," and Bush accused Clinton of lying about almost everything, saying, "If he's elected, he'll turn the White House into the Waffle House." Pat Robertson warned that the feminist movement—which he seemed to equate with the Democratic Party—"is a socialist, antifamily movement that encourages women to leave their husbands, kill their children, practice witchcraft, destroy capitalism, and become lesbians." Pat Buchanan, a staunch right-wing Republican candidate for the nomination during the primary campaign, abandoned his anti-Bush tactics long enough to charge that Clinton's foreign policy experience was "pretty much confined to having had breakfast once at the International House of Pancakes."

One certainly true charge made was that Clinton gave extremely long speeches. His nominating speech for Dukakis at the 1988 convention was, some said, interminable. ("It wasn't my finest hour," Clinton later said. "It wasn't even my finest hour and a half.") At the outset of his own acceptance speech, which was "only" fifty-three minutes long, he said, "I'm going to finish my [1988] speech." Senator John Danforth pointed out, "anyone who can speak for fifty-three minutes without saying a thing belongs in the Senate and not the White House."

Clinton also was charged with having a "twelve-year affair" with a woman named Gennifer Flowers, who surfaced long enough to sell her story to one of the gossip papers. This charge almost wrecked Clinton's candidacy, but he and his wife Hillary appeared on the television show *Sixty Minutes* and seemed to get the issue behind them. Throughout the campaign, however, there were references and jokes implying that Clinton was a womanizer. One such joke asked, "How is the election like *The Wizard of Oz*?" Answer: "Perot is looking for courage, Quayle is

" Each candidate will be allowed an opening sound-bite, then they may respond to questions with a memorable slogan or withering put-down, and finally have the chance for a closing zinger... "

(©1992 *The Record*, Jimmy Margulies.)

looking for a brain, Bush is looking for a heart, and Clinton is looking for Dorothy." The Clintonians had learned a lot from the Dukakis campaign, however. They had a team assembled in Little Rock to see that no Republican charge went unanswered, and their response time was almost zero.

Clinton's main difficulty dated back to 1969: He had evaded the draft during the Vietnam War. Bush said it wasn't evading the draft that was the issue—after all, Quayle had done so too—it was Clinton's lack of candor about the whole affair. Bush aides pointed out that "Slick Willie" [Clinton] had put out several stories, all different, about his draft status, and he had seemed to say he hadn't smoked marijuana, and then he said he did, "and I didn't like it and didn't inhale." They even implied that while he was a student at Oxford he had gone to Russia to plot against his country and had considered changing his citizenship to British. (The State Department was given the seemingly illegal assignment of checking out the latter charge.) In one of the presidential debates, Clinton equated Bush's character attacks with McCarthyism. "When Joe McCarthy went around the country attacking people's patriotism," he said, "a senator from Connecticut [Bush's own father, Prescott Bush] denounced him. Your father was right," and "you are wrong to attack my patriotism."

Bush apologized for breaking his no-tax pledge, saying it was "a mistake" forced on him by the Democrats. He now said he would never, ever raise taxes again. (An aide said that this was not a promise, however.) He then ran, ironically, as the candidate "you can trust." To counter Clinton's "time for a change" theme, Bush also ran as the candidate of change. This seemed implausible as well, since he was coming off twelve years of incumbency as president and vice president. The truth seemed to be, as one Bush insider put it, "We have no coordinated negative campaign, we have no positive campaign whatsoever, and we have no agenda for governing." Finally, Bush, like Reagan in 1984, ran as Harry Truman, which was in a way appropriate, considering how far behind he was in the polls.

Bush's relations with Reagan drew some notice also. In March Reagan reportedly said of Bush, "He doesn't seem to stand for anything," and, it was said, Reagan refused to be seen in public with him. One White House aide said, "Reagan was too senile to make an appearance," but another said, "Nancy made him do it." Mrs. Reagan was probably still smarting over Bush's earlier statement that George Deukmejian, not Reagan, was "the great governor of the State of California."

Clinton at times seemed to be running as Elvis Presley, one of his boyhood idols, prompting Bush to call the Clinton plan "Elvis Economics." If he wins, Bush said, "America will be checking into the 'Heartbreak Hotel.'" Jay Leno contributed his opinion that there was a difference between Elvis economics and Bush economics. "Elvis has been seen," he said, alluding to the many reported sightings of Elvis alive since his death in 1977.

For the most part, Clinton stuck to his main message: the state of the economy and the need for change. (A reporter who complained that the "change" incantation was boring, was told by a Clinton aide, "the point of the campaign is not to entertain journalists.") Bush told the voters that if Clinton won, "change is all you will have left in your pocket." James Carville, Clinton's campaign manager, kept his cool, however, and focused on the winning issue. Through it all he kept a sign in his office reading, "It's the economy, stupid!" (This apparently evolved from an Alcoholics Anonymous slogan, "Keep it simple, stupid," the *stupid* being added to make possible the acronym KISS.)

Perot bowed out of the race in July, observing that the Democrats seemed to have their act together. Perot's withdrawal, according to one reporter, was "the greatest missed opportunity since Napoleon failed to take Moscow." This was an odd observation, since Napoleon *took* Moscow, but no matter; Perot reentered the race in October.

Clinton and Perot changed presidential campaigning radically and perhaps permanently by appearing on commercial television talk shows such as *Larry King Live* rather than political talk shows like *Meet the Press*. Early in the campaign, when he seemed hopelessly behind both Bush and Perot, Clinton played the saxophone on *The Arsenio Hall Show*, prompting Arsenio to note how rare it was "to see a Democrat blowing something besides an election." Bush first refused to appear on the talk shows, but later relented, except, he said, for Hall's. "Well excuse me, George Herbert irregular-heart-beating, read-my-lying-lipping, slipping-in-the-polls, do-nothing, deficit-raising . . . Walker Bush," Arsenio replied, "I don't remember inviting [you] to my show."

Dan Quayle, of course, was the butt of numerous jokes, as he had been in 1988. Early on he took on Murphy Brown as having no sound family values. (She had nothing else, as well, since she was a fictional television character.) He also attended a spelling bee where he urged a sixth-grader, the eventual winner, to add an "e" to the end of the word "potato." "That's fine phonetically, but you're missing just a little bit," Quayle said. The student thought Quayle was missing more than a little bit, and later said the incident "showed the rumors about the vice president are true—that he's an idiot." A wag said that the student should agree to stop watching *Murphy Brown* if Quayle would start watching *Sesame Street*.

The campaign wound down with Clinton and Bush exchanging jabs and questioning each other's veracity. "Bush is just making all this up," Clinton said. On farming, "He and Quayle don't know sic 'em from sooey, and they're trying to tell farmers that I'll put them out of business." Perot seemed immune from attacks by the other two, since both of them were hoping in the end to get his voters. As president, he said, "I'll be like a mechanic who's under the hood, working on the engine." This reminded columnist George Will of William Howard Taft's listening to a young aide pontificate on the machinery of government. "He really thinks it's machinery," Taft said.

Clinton won the election with 370 electoral votes to 168 for Bush. Perot won no electoral votes, but as noted earlier, he got more popular votes than any independent candidate since Teddy Roosevelt in the Bull Moose campaign. Because of Perot's presence in the race, no candidate won a majority of the popular vote, but Clinton's was the highest of any Democrat in history. Both Bush and Quayle were magnanimous in defeat, with Quayle praising Clinton for his skillful campaigning and Bush inviting him to the White House for a smooth transition. Once again our system had made a peaceful transfer of power and "the torch" literally *was* "passed to a new generation."

In 1996 Bill Clinton became the first Democratic president since Franklin D. Roosevelt to win a second term. Clinton and his running mate, Vice President Al Gore, defeated the Republican slate of Senator Bob Dole and former representative Jack Kemp with a popular vote of 49 percent to 41 percent and 379 to 159 electoral votes. Ross Perot, who again ran as a third-party candidate, received 8 percent of the popular vote, about half of what he won in 1992.

Clinton promised in every speech, it seemed, to build a bridge to the twenty-first century. He was comfortably ahead in all the polls and evidently figured there was no reason for rocking the boat. Indeed, the election made it appear that Clinton and Dole actually liked each other. "Dole would make a better president," Clinton said, "than the rest of these jokers." Dole's jokes were less than vicious, and in many cases were directed at himself. For example, his wife Elizabeth, in her capacity as head of the Red Cross, had visited many disaster areas, Dole said, "not including my campaign." Generally, Dole's criticism was his continuous question, "Where's the outrage?" But after the election, Dole said of Clinton, "He was my opponent, not my enemy."

From the outset Dole had big disadvantages. He had to admit that he had voted against Medicare, and he was stuck with the Republican platform's "pro-life" or antiabortion plank. He dutifully kept the pro-life plank, but invited those who disagreed with it to vote for him anyway. "That's going too far," said one conservative.

The Republicans' main hope seemed to be to run on the character issue, but the public didn't seem to care. In April of 1996 a group of Republican pollsters watched a focus group talk about Clinton. They called him "slick" and "smooth," a draft dodger, adulterer, with a "big-mouth wife." And these were Clinton supporters! Why are we down fifteen points? the pollsters asked.

Several of Dole's supporters were willing to grant Clinton two terms, according to their signs: "First term in the White House. The second one in jail." Speaker of the House Newt Gingrich, who engineered the Republican takeover of the House and Senate in 1994, was harsher: "He [Clinton] was the biggest liar in the history of the [presidential] office." Gingrich didn't seem to like Dole either, having earlier labeled him "the tax collector for the welfare state."

In a surprise move, Dole resigned his Senate seat in the spring of 1996, hoping his leaving "the trappings of power" with "nothing to fall back on" would help his campaign. But nothing worked. His resignation, however, did allow him to say in his gracious concession speech, "Tomorrow will be the first time in my life I don't have anything to do."

Newsweek said Kennedy and Reagan had mastered the role of the presidency. Ford never managed it. Neither did Carter or George H.W. Bush. Clinton did. Frank Luntz, a Republican pollster, called him "the greatest communicator since FDR, better even than the Gipper." "Reagan was likeable," said Luntz. "People don't like Bill Clinton, and yet they follow him." This was like the compliment paid FDR once by a staunch Republican on the occasion of one of Roosevelt's coups: "We, who hate your gaudy guts, salute you."

The Clintonians realized early on that Gingrich was a liability for Dole, and, in the spirit of Reagan's 1984 mockery of Cartermondale, dubbed Dole "Dolegingrich." Because of his transparent attempt to help the rich by trying to cut Medicare by $270 billion and give a tax cut of $245 billion to the wealthier taxpayers, Gingrich, some said, was the "most hated man" in America. It didn't help any that the voters blamed him for shutting down the government in 1995 in a budget disagreement with Clinton. When it seemed evident that Clinton was headed

Dole campaign (Ann Telnaes, copyright 1996, Tribune Media
Services. Reprinted with permission.)

for a big win, Gingrich, fearing the loss of Congress, came up with the
subtle message, "Don't Give Clinton a Blank Check," which, of course,
scuttled Dole.

Dole exasperated many of his aides because of his independent
campaigning style. He also kept referring to the presidency as the
"presincy," prompting his speech coach to say, "Maybe we should run
for an office we can pronounce." Another disappointment with his team
was over supply-side economics, the theory that the government would
have more money by cutting taxes. Dole hated supply-side economics.
"A bus of supply-side economists fell off a cliff," quipped Dole. "The
bad news? Three seats were empty."

Dole's chief strategist, Bill Lacy, wanted him to run on the so-called
"three Rs": reining in the government, reconnecting the government to
our values, and reasserting American leadership abroad. Dole hated the
three Rs. Once on the Larry King Show he fumbled around trying to
spell out his message and finally said, shrugging, "whatever it is."

Bill Clinton left office in 2001 with what appeared to be a mixed legacy. He presided over the nation's longest economic expansion, with the unemployment and poverty rates dropping to their lowest levels in a generation. Stock investors were treated to the greatest bull market in history, as measured by the Dow-Jones industrial average's rise from 3,301 in January 1993, to 10,787 in January 2001. More importantly perhaps, the federal budget went from a deficit of $290 billion to a surplus of $237 billion.

To be fair, President Bush exhibited great statesmanship when he agreed to break his no-tax pledge. This probably destroyed his presidency but may have helped save the financial situation of the country. Clinton's deficit reduction bill of 1993, together with Bush's new taxes, led to the balanced budget. Not a single Republican voted with Clinton, which allowed him to claim credit for the first balanced budget (in 1998) since Lyndon Johnson's in 1969.

The flip side of the Clinton legacy, which led to his impeachment, was his sexual dalliance with a young White House intern, Monica Lewinsky. Although Clinton was exonerated (that is, not convicted) by the Senate, and finished his term with an approval rating of some 68 percent, higher even than the popular Reagan, history's verdict is still to be rendered.

Impeachment

I n the history of the American republic only two presidents, Andrew
Johnson and Bill Clinton, have been impeached. Richard Nixon
almost certainly would have been, as well, had he not resigned
instead. As noted in the chapter on Watergate, Nixon's alleged offenses
were deemed impeachable by the House Judiciary Committee. By then
his support in the Senate had disappeared, and he would very likely have
been removed from office had his case run its course. Johnson and
Clinton were both acquitted by the senators, who evidently felt that the
allegations against them did not rise to the level of impeachable offenses.

What then constitutes an impeachable offense? In Article II, Section 4
of the Constitution, the case for impeachment is provided for: "The
President, Vice-President, and all civil officers of the United States, shall
be removed from office on impeachment for, and conviction of, treason,
bribery, or other high crimes and misdemeanors." So, what are high
crimes and misdemeanors? George Mason, one of the founding fathers,
took the phrase to mean "political offenses against the state," its meaning
in English common law since the 1300s. (Scholars may recall, however,
that Mason looked down his nose at George Washington as an "upstart
surveyor," which might cause some to question his judgment. Alexander

The impeachment committee (Benjamin F. Butler at left; photograph by Mathew Brady).

Hamilton, however, held somewhat the same opinion on impeachment as Mason.) It should also be said that the word "misdemeanor" has evolved to mean a minor offense, but in the Framers' time high misdemeanors were offenses against the state.

In the mid-1970s when the Republicans were trying to get rid of Supreme Court Justice William O. Douglas, then-President Ford said, "an impeachable offense is whatever a majority of Congress considers" it "to be." If Ford is right, then no president is safe from a House with a rogue majority.

The so-called Radical Republicans in 1868 sensed that Andrew Johnson was planning to follow Lincoln's policy of clemency toward the South, and since they were in charge of both the House and Senate, they were determined to follow their own reconstruction policy. Toward that end, they passed the Tenure of Office Act, the main provision of which forbade the president's removing any member of his cabinet without the consent of the Senate.

Johnson held that the act was unconstitutional, as it certainly seemed to be, and as the Supreme Court found later, in 1887. He therefore immediately tested the act by firing Secretary of War Edwin M. Stanton. General U. S. Grant succeeded Stanton, but when the Radicals got up in arms, he vacated the office. Stanton moved back in and locked the door. This seemed to be a more impeachable act than Johnson's, but no one appeared to care. On February 24, 1868, the House impeached Johnson by a vote of 126 to 47. Ten of the eleven articles of impeachment had to do with Stanton and the other consisted of garbled newspaper reports of Johnson's speeches. To show their compassion, one supposes, the Radicals left out the monstrous charge that Johnson was an accessory to Lincoln's murder. Even with this concession, the historian Samuel Eliot Morison labeled the impeachment of Johnson "one of the most disgraceful episodes in our history."

With Chief Justice Salmon P. Chase presiding, the Senate began Johnson's trial. General Benjamin F. Butler, "now uglier and paunchier than ever" (according to Morison), presented the Radicals' case, promising from the outset to conduct the proceedings as he "would a horse thievery case, and I know how to do that." A member of Johnson's able defense pointed out that if the Radicals succeed, "you settle that hereafter a party having a sufficient majority in the House and Senate can depose the President of the United States. The Radicals retorted that Johnson was "the greatest criminal of our age and country," and "an incubus and a disgrace."

With Butler in charge, the proceedings were farcical. He attempted to make Johnson's witnesses appear ridiculous. As an example, at one point a witness started to testify on something Johnson had told him one afternoon at five o'clock. At that point Butler halted his testimony, saying that at that time of the day Johnson would be too drunk to speak coherently.

There were fifty-four senators judging Johnson—forty-two Republicans and twelve Democrats. A two-thirds vote was required for conviction, which meant the Republicans needed at least thirty-six. May 16 was the day of decision, and the eleventh article of impeachment, which encompassed all the others, was taken up first. The vote was thirty-five to nineteen, and thus Johnson was not convicted. The other articles were either voted on with the same result or were dropped.

"He's supported by Secretary Seward" (an unfair depiction of Andrew Johnson drunk/ *Petroleum V. Nasby*).

Seven courageous Republicans had voted with the Democrats, and thus Johnson survived.

When his term was over and without attending the inauguration of his successor, General Grant, Johnson left Washington and retired to his hometown of Greeneville, Tennessee. Eight years earlier a banner was strung across its main street reading, "Andrew Johnson, Traitor." On his retirement a banner was strung up, as well, but it read, "Andrew Johnson, Patriot."

In 1875 Andrew Johnson was elected to the Senate, the only former president to serve there.

Bill Clinton did not have the "honeymoon" with the press that new presidents typically enjoy. Instead, upon taking office he was confronted immediately with charges that he and his wife, Hillary, had committed some unspecified crime in connection with a fifteen-year-old land deal known as Whitewater. In just a year after Clinton took office, Robert Fiske, a moderate Republican, was appointed special prosecutor to investigate the charges. Besides Whitewater, these had grown to include "hairgate," "Fostergate," "travelgate," "filegate," and "troopergate." (Hairgate was a presidential haircut at the Los Angeles airport, while supposedly, but not actually, holding up air traffic. Fostergate was a charge that Vince Foster, a Clinton friend, had not committed suicide, as it seemed clear that he

(Rob Rogers. Reprinted by permission of United Feature Syndicate, Inc.)

had, but that he was murdered, presumably because he knew damaging things about Whitewater. Travelgate referred to an administration attempt to fire some or all of the White House travel employees. Filegate had to do with some FBI files discovered in the White House. Troopergate was a theory that some state troopers knew of affairs by Clinton when he was governor of Arkansas.)

A three-judge panel, known as the Special Division, in effect, fired Fiske in August 1994, to avoid "the appearance of impropriety." They then hired Kenneth Starr, an outspoken Republican opponent of Clinton. (One of the judges had lunch with two staunch Republican senators just two weeks prior to the appointment, but they never discussed the Whitewater case, it was said. They talked of old friends and prostate problems.) Starr then began a five-year, $50 million pursuit of Clinton, which former Senator Dale Bumpers compared to that of Inspector Javert's relentless hounding of Jean Valjean in *Les Misérables*, which lasted throughout most of that lengthy book.

Clinton was also charged with having sexual affairs, ranging from groping to raping huge numbers of women. There were so many that it became necessary to identify some of them as Jane Doe number 3, Jane Doe number 4, and so on. He must have been the greatest presidential Don Juan since Grover Cleveland, who, it may be recalled, had "victimized countless women now married" and was "alarmed lest their relations with him be exposed." Clinton's main competitor in this regard would seem, however, to be Warren G. Harding, who actually sired a child with a young lady named Nan Britton in an Oval Office closet. In Clinton's case, a frightening moment for a weary public must have come toward the end of the investigation when Starr hinted that he was considering extending his seemingly endless probe by calling as a witness Jane Doe number 5.

One of the earliest charges leveled at Clinton was in a lawsuit brought by Paula Jones, who was identified at first only as "Paula." She claimed that he had sexually harassed her by crudely propositioning her in an Arkansas hotel room while he was governor, and that she was filing the suit to recover her good name. At this, ex-Senator George McGovern pointed out that since no one knew her or her name, she was the one responsible for publicizing it. The Clinton lawyers tried to get her suit postponed until the end of his administration, but the Supreme Court refused to allow it, a decision the noted lawyer Vincent Bugliosi

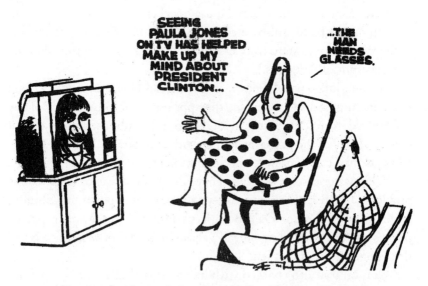

(Reprinted with permission, Steve Kelley, *The Times Picayune*.)

called "idiotic on its face." Only Justice Breyer seemed to think that it might interfere with the president's ability to carry out his official duties. "Boy, was he ever right," said columnist David Broder, a year later.

The presiding judge eventually threw out the Jones case, and Clinton settled with her lawyers, no doubt to prevent the courts from reinstating the case. First, however, the discovery process discovered Monica Lewinsky, a young White House intern with whom Clinton had carried on a sexual dalliance from November 1995 until March 1997. Then Lewinsky, of course, was discovered by Kenneth Starr.

The sexual relationship was apparently oral sex and stopped short of intercourse. At his deposition in the Jones case, Clinton took advantage of the definition of sex as given by Jones's lawyers to say that "I did not have sexual relations with that woman, Ms. Lewinsky." At his grand jury deposition, Clinton admitted that he "engaged in conduct that was wrong," but said his actions "did not constitute sexual relations as I understood that term to be defined at my January . . . deposition."

Hand on the Bible, 1997 (Ed Stein. Reprinted with permission of *Rocky Mountain News*.)

An interesting exchange followed. Prosecutor: "the statement [of Bob Bennett's] that there was no sex of any kind . . . was an utterly false statement. Is that correct?" Clinton: "It depends on what the definition of 'is' is. If the—if the—if 'is' means is and never has been, that is not—that is one thing. If it means there is none, that was a completely true statement." Clinton's rationale for this comical statement was that Bob Bennett was Clinton's lawyer; Clinton wasn't Bennett's. Why should the client monitor his lawyer?

Starr's report to the House of Representatives was 452 pages long and was accompanied by thirty-six boxes of supporting material—eighteen boxes for each party. A cover letter was sent specifying that the contents of the referral may not be publicly disclosed unless authorized by the House. This, of course, was an invitation by Starr to the Representatives to make the report public. This they did, before anyone had a chance to read it.

Starr also had a blue dress of Lewinsky's stained with Clinton's semen, established by a DNA test.

On November 19, 1998, Starr spent twelve hours testifying before the Judiciary Committee presenting his report and answering questions. Very little new information came out except Starr's acknowledgement that several months earlier he had found no grounds to bring charges against the Clintons with regard to Whitewater, Travelgate, or Filegate. (He had already agreed that Vince Foster was a suicide.) In other words, all he had was Lewinsky. Representative Barney Frank, and later the *New York Times*, denounced him for not revealing this changed situation before the November 3 elections. He also failed to mention Lewinsky's adamant testimony that "no one ever asked me to lie and I was never promised a job for my silence."

Thus William Ginsburg, Lewinsky's first lawyer, was proved to be right when he wrote in an open letter in May, "congratulating" Mr. Starr for his "callous disregard for cherished constitutional rights," which "may have succeeded in unmasking a sexual relation between two consenting adults."

On December 19, 1998, the House of Representatives, in a near-party-line vote, impeached the president. By 228 to 206, the House accused him of perjury and by 221 to 212, of obstruction of justice.

Clinton's polls (Jeff MacNelly. Copyright 1998, Tribune Media Services. Reprinted with permission).

An interesting sidelight occurred on October 4, 1998, when Larry Flynt, the publisher of *Hustler* magazine, announced he would pay $1 million to any woman willing to go public about any affairs they had had with a current member of the U.S. Congress or a high-ranking government official. In a short time, two thousand women answered the ad. By the time of the election on November 3, the list had been pared down to twelve women, one of whom had fingered Republican Bob Livingston. The election was a disaster for the Republicans. Gingrich had predicted a twenty-seat gain earlier in the day, but Democrats held their own in the Senate and gained five seats in the House. In a stunning move, Gingrich resigned as Speaker and later resigned from the House. It later surfaced that Gingrich had been engaged in a longtime sexual affair with a young congressional aide that was very similar to Clinton's tryst with Lewinsky. On December 17, Livingston, who was then the Speaker-designate, disclosed that he had "been outed by Larry Flynt." Following Gingrich's example, he too resigned from Congress.

(Jim Berry. Reprinted by permission of Newspaper Enterprise Association, Inc.)

Later Flynt was asked if he had any regrets about offering money for stories. No, he said. "There's nothing that changes people's moral outlook like money."

Clinton's trial by the Senate began January 7, 1999, with Chief Justice William Rehnquist presiding. The trial itself was anticlimactic because polls consistently showed Clinton's approval rating at 65 to 70 percent and Starr's below 10 percent. Also, Republicans suffered in the ratings, which got worse as the trial progressed. Thus they wanted to end the proceedings as soon as possible. The House managers (those charged with prosecuting the trial) were told by their leader, Representative Henry Hyde, "We're an annoyance . . . in the bosom of this great body."

The public grew weary of the trial as well. Toward the end, a spectator suddenly jumped up and shouted, "Good God Almighty! Take the vote and get it over with."

On February 12, 1999, the Senate acquitted President Clinton on both articles of impeachment. On perjury the vote was forty-five guilty

History (*Seattle Post Intelligencer* 1999 / Steve Greenberg, reprinted with permission).

and fifty-five not guilty, and on obstruction of justice the vote was fifty-fifty, both of which fell well short of the sixty-seven needed to convict.

Many of Clinton's enemies blamed the American public for his acquittal. Paul Weyrich, who coined the term Moral Majority, said there was no longer a moral majority. William J. Bennett, a noted author and, some said, a self-appointed authority on the nation's virtues, said ordinary Americans were complicit in Clinton's corruption. "I will not defend the public," he said. Finally Senator Robert C. Smith's wife could not believe the opinion polls that supported the president. They must have been taken of "people coming out of Hooters [a chain of restaurants with scantily clad waitresses] on Saturday night," she said. Representative Bob Barr cleared it all up. "Real Americans" favored conviction, he said.

In defense of Clinton's job as president, columnist Glenn Feldman wrote that, "As president, his record is almost embarrassingly superior to anyone in recent memory. One has to go back at least to the Great Depression to find his equal."

"On the other hand," says Feldman, "there is very little that can be said in defense of Bill Clinton's conduct with regard to Monica Lewinsky. He engaged in a sexual affair with a twenty-one-year-old. He lied to his wife, his friends, his cabinet, and the American people. Such is not the stuff of which anyone can be proud."

A question begs to be asked about Clinton. His enemies, with their unlimited resources and authority, were relentless in watching every move he made. Why then was he so reckless? He squandered his last two years in office, which could have been his best.

The Election from Hell

The coming of the year 2000, known affectionately as Y2K, was dreaded by many throughout 1999 as the year ushering in the millennium. It was the last year of the twentieth century, but many thought it was the first year of the twenty-first, and that it would bring with it untold miseries. It was said that the major Y2K problem was that 65 percent of computers were not programmed to deal with four-digit dates, so 2000 would be represented by 00. Social Security checks could not be issued, the transportation system would be disabled, food and water supplies would be curtailed, and there would be nothing on television.

There were religious fears, as well, but nothing like the fear in the millennial year 1000 (Y1K), when Christians around the world were told in Revelation 20:1–3 that the Devil would be released that year after one thousand years in captivity. To make matters worse, the pope, Sylvester II, was French, and was interested in mathematics and Arabic numbers. He was "the first millennium's Bill Gates," according to authors Robert Lacey and Danny Danziger.

None of these terrible predictions came true, of course, but Y2K struck at the end of the year in the form of the Presidential Election from Hell. It was also known as the election that would not die. Indeed, it lasted from November 7 until December 12, when the Supreme Court put it out of its misery.

In 2000 America was enjoying the greatest economic expansion in history, the unemployment rate had dropped to 3.9 percent, the lowest in thirty years, crime rates had plummeted, and the cold war was over; in fact, the Soviet Union no longer existed. The United States reigned alone as the world's only superpower, and it had the most powerful military machine relative to any other country in the world, indeed in the history of the world. This included the Roman legions at their peak, the British Empire when the sun never set on it, Hitler's Wehrmacht, and the minions of Alexander the Great.

Also in 2000 Tiger Woods won the U.S. Open by fifteen strokes over his nearest opponent, the largest margin of victory ever in a major golf tournament. The New York Yankees won the World Series over the New York Mets in the first "Subway Series" since the days when the Dodgers and Giants were in New York. It was the fourth world championship for the Yanks in the last five years. Pete Sampras won a record-breaking thirteenth Grand Slam tennis title, defeating Patrick Rafter at Wimbledon. Elizabeth, the Queen Mother, turned 100, *American Beauty* won the Academy Award for best picture, baseball star Alex Rodriguez signed a ten-year contract with the Texas Rangers for $252 million, and comedian Dennis Miller was hired as a commentator on *Monday Night Football*. Scientists announced the deciphering of the human genome, one of the most significant advances ever made in biology, and Hillary Clinton was elected U.S. Senator from New York, the first presidential wife to seek public office from the White House.

The two candidates in the 2000 election were Democrat Al Gore, Clinton's vice president, and Republican George W. Bush, governor of Texas and son of former president George Herbert Walker Bush. Writer Jake Tapper unkindly gave them other names. Gore, he said, was "an uninspiring technocrat politician," who was "cold and ruthless." Bush, he claimed, was a "brilliant schmoozer and deft liar," with "the intellectual inquisitiveness of your average fern." Columnist Robert J. Samuelson was content to infer that Gore was "a liar" and Bush "an imbecile." The worst take on either candidate, however, was that of Ron Reagan, son of

PARTY SYMBOLS

REPUBLICAN
ELEPHANT

DEMOCRATIC
DONKEY

REFORM
LOON

Party Symbols (*The Des Moines Register*/Brian Duffy).

Ronald, who said of Bush, "He's probably the least qualified person ever nominated by a major party. . . . What is his accomplishment? That he's no longer an obnoxious drunk?"

Both candidates had opposition in the primaries. Ex-senator and ex-basketball superstar Bill Bradley challenged Gore, but made little headway, and withdrew on March 9. Bush's opponent, Senator John McCain, however, was a different story. Bush had hoped to run as a "compassionate conservative," which angered one conservative Republican who thought it implied that conservatives in general were not compassionate. But no matter. When McCain, the Vietnam War hero and ex-POW, surprisingly and convincingly won the New Hampshire primary, Bush changed his tactics and ran as a "reformer with results."

The campaigning also turned negative, with the Bushies attacking McCain as "a hypocrite," "a liar," "a thief," and "a cheat." They even

"I'm a compassionate conservative . . . so in addition to 'GET LOST,'
I'd like to add, 'HAVE A NICE DAY.' "

Compassionate Conservative, 1999 (Bruce Beattie, Copley News Service).

branded him a "liberal," the final insult in the Republican lexicon. One
Bush supporter said that McCain was no hero but a Manchurian can-
didate, brainwashed and sent home to betray his comrades in arms.
Another called Mrs. McCain a drug addict and a weirdo. For his
part, McCain attacked Bush's claim to be a reformer. "If he's a reformer,"
McCain said, "I'm an astronaut."

Unfortunately for McCain, his success rallied Bush's conservative
base. Also, the later primary voters were more purely Republican, in contrast with those of New Hampshire with its large independent contin-
gent. Thus when McCain singled out the Reverend Pat Robertson as an
"evil influence" on the Republican Party, he could kiss the South
Carolina primary goodbye.

McCain won his home state of Arizona and pulled off another surprise by taking Michigan, but after that began a continuous slide. He
withdrew on March 9, the same day Bradley withdrew from the
Democratic race.

Interestingly, some analysts thought the primary elections turned against McCain because of an ad he ran comparing Bush to Clinton, stating that both stretched the truth. Voters, they believed, felt it was wrong for a candidate to attack a member of his or her own party this way. McCain quickly pulled the ad.

Many Republican leaders disliked McCain. Haley Barbour, for instance, complained on a talk show that the press was "slobbering" over McCain. "Guilty as charged," replied columnist Mary McGrory. "He talks to us, returns our calls, says things he shouldn't, takes them back, and doesn't blame anyone else. This is novel for us."

Bush chose as his running mate Dick Cheney, former White House chief of staff and former secretary of defense. This seemed a good move because Cheney had experience in foreign and domestic matters that Bush lacked. Gore selected Connecticut Senator Joe Lieberman, said to be a dramatic choice since it made Lieberman the first Jewish major-party nominee in American history. Lieberman would energize Jewish voters in states like Florida and would help distance Gore from the Clinton scandals. (Lieberman was one of the few Democratic senators to condemn Clinton for his Lewinsky caper.)

At the Republican convention, held in Philadelphia, Cheney delivered a harshly partisan speech invoking the Clinton-Gore mantra of 1992: "It's time for them to go." In answer to the Democrats' claim of responsibility for "the longest economic expansion in American history," the Republicans credited Presidents Reagan and the elder Bush for hammering "into place the framework for today's prosperity and surplus." Also, the demise of the Soviet Union took place during their administrations, not Clinton's.

The Republicans attempted to shed the party's right-wing image with their "compassionate conservative" claim and by their "inclusion" of a number of African Americans and Hispanics at the speakers' podium. This latter feat required some work because it had to be done without alienating their conservative base. Critics pointed out that their minority delegates constituted only 8 percent of the total, whereas the Democrats in their convention two weeks later had a 35 percent minority group. This "inclusion illusion" provoked claims of "phony," with Lieberman saying, "Not since Tom Hanks won an Oscar has there been that much acting in Philadelphia."

(Rob Rogers. reprinted by permission of United Feature Syndicate, Inc.)

Since Bush had been tagged constantly as an inept orator, friend and foe alike anxiously awaited his acceptance speech. Contrary to expectations, he delivered a "very presidential" address. "This administration had its moment," he said. "They had their chance. They have not led. We will."

The Republicans thus left their convention with a unified party and a substantial bounce in the polls.

The Democratic convention was held in Los Angeles and began with Bill Clinton as the featured speaker. He electrified the crowd with a recital of the accomplishments of the Clinton-Gore administration: the long economic expansion, plummeting crime rates, low inflation, easy credit, huge deficits replaced by huge surpluses, and the remarkable stock market performance. After his speech he left Los Angeles, some said to the relief of the Gore forces, many of whom wanted to see the vice president get out of Clinton's shadow and be his own man. Upon Clinton's departure, one journalist said, "Elvis has left the building"; . . . now we will see if the Democrats' "new headliner can fill the void."

(Rob Rogers. reprinted by permission of United Feature Syndicate, Inc.)

Before Gore began his own speech on the last night of the convention, he embraced his wife Tipper, and planted The Kiss, a long, passionate signal that, unlike some people, he was faithful to his wife. He also gave a highly competent acceptance speech, which together with The Kiss gave him his largest lead in the polls.

Two other conventions that were to have monumental effects on the 2000 election were that of the Reform Party, the remnants of Ross Perot's minions of 1992 and 1996, and that of the Green Party, headed by environmentalist Ralph Nader. In a bizarre turn of events, Republican Pat Buchanan became the standard bearer of the Reform Party. It was assumed that Nader would hurt Gore in the general election, and that Buchanan would hurt Bush, but in fact each would deal Gore's hopes a body blow.

During the postconvention campaign, Al Gore was in a dilemma. Should he hitch his wagon to Clinton's star and run on the amazingly good economic record, or should he distance himself from Clinton and the Lewinsky scandal and the impeachment, and run as his own man?

Gore vs. Bush and Nader (*Gainesville Sun*/Jake Fuller).

He had plenty of advice as to which course to take, and in the end he was criticized by supporters and enemies on both sides of the issue. A Clinton aide said, "Gore's campaign is trying to make Bill Clinton their primary opponent. That is absolutely nutty." Others said the country was suffering from "Clinton fatigue," and Gore should run his own campaign. Karl Rove, Bush's top strategist, was grateful, he said, that Gore hadn't focused more on the nation's "extraordinary peace and prosperity." We should have gotten our brains beat out, he said.

A major criticism aimed at Gore during the campaign was that, while he was intelligent and well informed, he went to great pains to show his superiority. In the debates he was said to embellish his answers unnecessarily and roll his eyes and sigh audibly while Bush spoke. Gore, in answering a question from the press, even had the audacity to declare the great French novelist Stendhal to be his favorite author. Stendhal! Nobody could even *spell* Stendhal. The *New York Times* couldn't spell

Stendhal, as it turned out. (This was the second appearance of Stendhal in U.S. presidential politics. He also authored the line, "Speech was given to man to enable him to conceal his thoughts," which, it may be recalled, was used to discredit Martin Van Buren in the 1840 election.) Bush, of course, played it safer. His favorite book was said to be *The Hungry Caterpillar*, a children's story that he used to read to his kids. To be sure he wasn't seen as uppity, one supposes, as he had a dog named Spot!

One other example of Gore's knowledge being used against him was his exchange with Bush over the need for an HMO reform bill. This occurred in the last of the three debates, where Bush seemed to agree with Gore on the desirability of such a bill, whereupon Gore stated that he was for the Dingell-Norwood bill being debated by Congress, and asked Bush if he also favored it. It was never clear if Bush favored Dingell-Norwood or not, or if he was even familiar with it. The following Sunday morning on ABC's "This Week," Sam Donaldson and Cokie Roberts could not contain their glee over something about the bill. It may have been Gore's identifying the bill correctly, or perhaps Representative John Dingell's name struck them as funny. Whatever their problem was, their audience received little or no information about what the bill said. Roberts said that what was important was not what the bill provided but "what comes across when you're watching the debate is this guy [presumably Gore] from Washington doing Washington-speak."

Throughout the three debates, and indeed through most of the campaign, Bush managed to keep his expectations low so that he always seemed to give a good account of himself. Also, he was fortunate that Gore spent a good deal of time on the character issue, which kept him off the robust economy.

Another Republican strategy was to make fun of Gore during the entire campaign on a number of bogus claims they charged him with making. One of these was the charge that he—Gore—claimed to have invented the Internet. What he did was take the lead in passing legislation to convert the then-current military communications system into the present Internet. Even Newt Gingrich vouched for Gore's role in the development of the Internet. Gore was never credited with what he did. He was always called the inventor of the Internet, followed by guffaws.

Both Bush and Gore were guilty of numerous gaffes in the campaign. Gore's were used to discredit him and make him out a liar. Bush's, on the other hand, mostly evoked smiles and were then forgotten, as when in an attack on Gore as a big-spending liberal, he blurted out that, "They want the federal government controlling Social Security like it's some kind of federal program!" On another occasion, it was discovered that a Republican ad attacking Gore's Medicare prescription drug plan included a split-second flash of the word "RATS," a slur on the last part of the Democrats' name. Bush denied the intent to send subliminal messages, which he repeatedly referred to as "subliminable."

These were petty attacks, but with less than a week to go in the campaign, a serious story broke. Bush, at age 30, had been arrested for drunk driving in Maine in 1976. Since this charge had been carefully covered up, it would seem to be a disaster for Bush's campaign of "character counts" against Clinton and Gore. This was especially true since a reporter came forward with the charge that Bush had lied to him in denying that the incident had ever happened. Bush's communications director, Karen Hughes, met the press first and observed that drinking and

Bush speaking (Mike Peters © Grimmy Inc. Distributed by King Features Syndicate).

driving was a mistake, and hoped that this event "would not have an impact in the final days of this election." Hughes and later Bush himself attempted to place the blame on whoever uncovered the story. "I do find it interesting," he said, "that it's come out four or five days before an election." Hughes agreed. "I think the Democrats owe the American people an explanation," she said.

Of course, the media should have found the story of George Bush's 1976 arrest for drunken driving. They had no excuse for not finding it, and as Katie Couric, of the *Today Show,* put it, "Given that reporters have been looking for years at the governor's background, why did they never find this before?"

At least one comedian noticed the Bush DUI. Jay Leno, on the *Tonight Show,* started his monologue with, "What's new with George Anheuser Bush?"

One issue that played a prominent role in the previous three elections, but was missing in 2000, was avoidance of military service by one

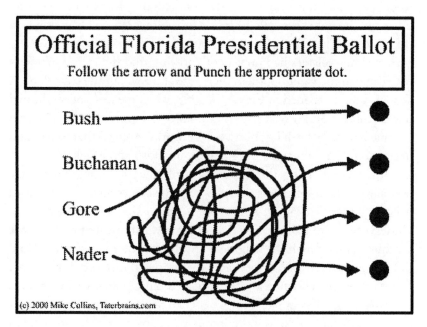

"Official" Florida ballot (Taterbrains.com/Mike Collins).

or more of the candidates. In particular, Bill Clinton and Dan Quayle were mercilessly pounded by the press for dodging the draft. Gore and Lieberman both served, but Cheney once told a reporter that he "had other priorities in the '60s than military service."

George W. Bush, as reported by the *Boston Globe* and later the *Toronto Star* (Linda McQuaig, November 2002), had "an embarrassing military past." He was allowed to enlist in the Texas National Guard during the Vietnam War, but during his tenure he asked for and received a transfer to the Alabama National Guard, and "never showed up for duty there," according to the commander and his assistant. He "could be classified as, at best, 'absent without leave (AWOL)' or, at worst, as an army deserter."

Why then did the press and the television medium overlook the draft-dodging issue in 2000? Some journalists attributed it to "alleged exhaustion." Perhaps they were resting so as to be ready if Clinton or Quayle ever ran again.

On election night, November 7, it became clear that Gore would win the popular vote by approximately half a million, and that Florida would play a key role in the vote that counted: the electoral college vote. Early on, the networks called Florida for Gore, presumably giving him the election. The call was based on the exit polls, which were probably correct. The pollsters had no way of knowing that thousands of voters who came in the front door had their votes thrown out the back door. A similar thing happened in Florida in 1988, when the exit polls indicated that Democrat Buddy MacKay had won the Senate race with Republican Connie Mack. In both elections, the networks reversed themselves and declared the winners to be the Republicans Bush and Mack.

All this is not to say that fraud was involved in the voting. There were basically two kinds of ballots not counted by machines used in punch-card balloting or written ballots. These were so-called *undervotes* and *overvotes*. Undervotes were ballots in which no vote was indicated because the machine didn't punch the ballot effectively, the voter was confused and didn't punch the ballot, or perhaps deliberately didn't vote for anyone. Overvotes occurred when a voter indicated more than one choice. This could happen, for example, if the voter tried to erase a name and vote for another name, or perhaps write in one name, mark it out, and write in another. It was estimated by the *Miami Herald*, in a report conducted after the election, that in Florida in 2000, some 174,000 votes were tossed out, about three percent of the total. In Gadsden County, Florida's only predominantly black county, an astonishing 12.4 percent of all ballots were thrown out. A hand count, provided for in Florida in close elections, would have counted many of the undervotes and overvotes, since the intent of the voter was often quite clear to a hand counter but not necessarily to a machine.

The networks not only reversed themselves once, they reversed themselves three times on election night. After declaring Gore the winner, they changed their decision to too close to call. (This must have vexed newscaster Dan Rather, who had said earlier, "When we call a state, you can bank on it.") They then declared Bush the winner. At this point Bush had a lead of less than 1,800 votes, and Gore called Bush, privately conceding the election. In spite of such a small Bush lead, Gore was on his way to the War Memorial Plaza in Nashville to formally concede when the networks changed their prognosis again to too close to call. By then, Bush's lead was less than 200 out of nearly six million votes.

At this point, in Bush's words, "Gore unconceded." He noted to Bush that "circumstances have changed dramatically since I first called you. Florida is too close to call." Bush explained that the networks were right, and to prove it, "Jeb's right here." "Your *little brother* doesn't get to make that call," said Gore.

The disenfranchisement of thousands of his voters was not the only setback for Gore. In Palm Beach county, a Jewish stronghold, a facing-page or so-called "butterfly" ballot, was used which diverted 3,407 votes from Gore to Pat Buchanan. "Those were not my votes," Buchanan said. "They were almost certainly intended for Al Gore." "The ballot is confusing," he added. "There's Bush and Gore as the first and second names on the left, but if you vote for the second dot, you vote for me, and my name's on the right. . . . I think they voted for me mistakenly."

"Jews for Buchanan. That's a joke, right?" said author John Nichols. It does strain one's credulity to believe that elderly Jewish voters would vote en masse for the one candidate most likely to be accused of anti-Semitism. This is especially true in a year when one of the major-party slates had a Jewish candidate for the first time in history.

The Bushies, however, felt that they could not concede that *any* votes were diverted from Gore, so they sent their spokesman, Ari Fleischer, to claim with a straight face that, "Palm Beach County is a Pat Buchanan stronghold."

Another problem for Gore was Ralph Nader's candidacy. A well-known environmentalist, as was Gore, Nader had no interest in seeing Bush elected president, or so it would seem. To the Democrats and also to his friends, who entreated him to withdraw, however, he refused. "Only Al Gore can beat Al Gore," said Nader, "And he's been doing a pretty good job of that." In an election that was a virtual tie between Bush and Gore, Nader got 2.7 million votes nationwide and 97,488 votes in Florida, nearly all of which were diverted from Gore.

On November 9, Florida Secretary of State Katherine Harris ordered the automatic machine recount, which showed Bush leading by 327 votes. Harris was also a co-chairman of the Bush campaign in Florida, and she spent the rest of the election struggle trying to certify a Bush victory.

The Republican strategy for winning the election was to get ahead, officially somehow, and to stay ahead by not allowing any manual recounts. They had Harris issuing rulings and standing by to certify any Bush election numbers, and they recruited James A. Baker III, former secretary of state, to use the courts to block any attempted hand counts.

One of Baker's tasks was to counter the Democrats' argument that "We should count all the votes," meaning, of course, to include the ones that had been thrown out, and thus not counted. "We need a strategy," Baker said. "No one can argue that we shouldn't count all the votes." His solution was that "the votes have been counted twice," and the Democrats want to keep counting until they get it to suit themselves.

The Democratic strategy was to take advantage of Florida law to recount the votes of selected counties where Gore was strong and where there were a large number of overvotes and undervotes.

On November 9 Gore asked for manual recounts in three, and later four, counties. Bush (that is, Baker) then filed suit in federal district court on November 11 to stop the manual recounts, which the court refused to do.

At this point, Harris issued opinions that the deadline for election certification would be in one day (November 14), and that manual

(By permission of Mike Luckovich and Creators Syndicate, Inc.)

recounts would not be permitted. This action, of course, required Gore to sue, which Baker found to be a sad day "when, for the first time in modern history, a candidate resorts to lawsuits to overturn the outcome of an election for president." He apparently felt no remorse about the suit he filed for Bush on November 11.

Once the lawsuits started, they dominated the proceedings. Gore was fighting to count ballots, and the Florida Supreme Court decided repeatedly, by a four-to-three vote, in his favor. The U.S. Supreme Court, on the other hand, sided with Bush by a five-to-four vote, to knock down every decision of the Florida Supremes. Some said the U.S. Supreme Court had no business interfering with a state's election, and they kept the Florida Supreme Court from doing its work. The Bushies simply reiterated their claim that the votes had already been counted—twice.

Bush had another thing going for him besides the lawyers. On November 22, a large group of Republican protesters (or thugs, as the Democrats called them) descended on the vote counters in Miami-Dade, demanding that the recounting end. The protesters were Washington

Who knows? (*Rockford Register-Star*/Bruce Quast).

employees of Republican congressmen, and they effectively stopped the recounts. Because they were well dressed, their performance was known as the "Brooks Brothers riot."

The networks' premature call that Bush had won Florida was in the end a disaster for Gore. As the deadlock wore on, and Baker's strategy of keeping Bush ahead by preventing recounts continued to work, the public came to perceive Gore as the challenger and a poor loser trying to steal the election. The man who had won the popular vote and who clearly was the choice of the majority of voters attempting to vote in Florida, was being asked even by his friends to concede. This was true even as polls showed the public willing to get the vote right as opposed to rushing the process.

Harris continued to throw up roadblocks. On November 26, she "certified" Bush the winner in Florida by 537 votes and denied the request for more time. The legal battle continued. On December 8 the

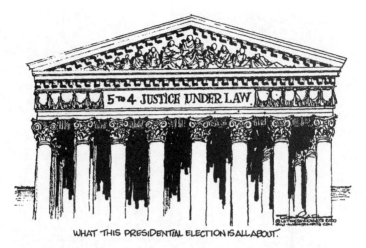

WHAT THIS PRESIDENTIAL ELECTION IS ALL ABOUT.

Paul Conrad (Copyright 2000, Tribune Media Services. Reprinted with permission).

Florida Supreme Court for the last time ruled that Gore's recounts could continue. "My God," thought a Gore aide, "We're really going to win." But the U.S. Supreme Court stopped the recount the very next day. The five most conservative members of the Court, William Rehnquist, Antonin Scalia, Clarence Thomas, Sandra Day O'Connor, and Anthony Kennedy, voted to stay the recount on the grounds that counting votes threatened irreparable harm to Bush. Justice John Paul Stevens, in the minority with Justices David Souter, Stephen Breyer, and Ruth Bader Ginsburg, thought that "counting every legally cast vote cannot constitute irreparable harm." It was no doubt true that continuing to count might cause harm to Bush, but not continuing to count might cause equal harm to Gore.

On December 12, the U.S. Supreme Court, by the same five-to-four vote, rejected further manual recounts, awarding the presidency to Bush. They did this in spite of Bush's spokesman, Joe Klock, on the previous day calling Justice Stevens, Justice Brennan (who had died in 1997), and Justice Souter, Justice Breyer. The ruling was that "The recount process . . . is inconsistent with the minimum procedures necessary to protect the fundamental right of each voter," and "It is evident that any recount seeking to meet the December 12 date will be unconstitutional." "In other

Do Blame Me (*Marin Independent Journal* 2000/Steve Greenberg, reprinted with permission).

words," columnist Tom Scarritt said, "any recount had to be finished by December 12. And any recount that was finished by December 12 would be unconstitutional." It was ten o'clock at night on December 12 when the Court issued its decision. That gave Gore two hours to recount ballots unconstitutionally.

The Court majority issued a *per curiam* (unsigned) report of their ruling. Attorney Vincent Bugliosi suggested that they didn't have the nerve to sign it. He also said that the Court had "committed one of the biggest and most serious crimes this nation has ever seen—pure and simple, the theft of the presidency . . . the perpetrators of this crime *have* to be denominated criminals."

The Court did not want their ruling to serve as a precedent. "Our consideration is limited to the present circumstances, for the problem of equal protection in election processes generally presents many complexities," the justices wrote. Amen to that! They had managed to block repeatedly Gore's efforts to have a recount, provided for by

Florida law, and now, the time had run out. Of the thirty-five days between the election and the awarding of the election to Bush, only three days were spent in which the votes of all the disputed counties were being recounted.

Justice Stevens, in his dissent, said, "Although we may never know with complete certainty the identity of the winner of this year's presidential election, the identity of the loser is perfectly clear. It is the nation's confidence in the judge as an impartial guardian of the rule of law." Mary McGrory said, "Antonin Scalia . . . might as well have been wearing a Bush button on his robes." Placards began appearing: "The President Select," "The People Have Spoken—All Five of Them," "Hail to the Thief," "Don't Blame Me. I Think I Voted for Gore, and a year or so later, a "Reelect Gore" bumper sticker. The other side had their placards as well, the leading one being "Sore Loserman," a play on the Democrats' "Gore Lieberman."

Gore gave a gracious concession speech. "Just moments ago, I spoke with George W. Bush and congratulated him on becoming the forty-third president of the United States," he said. "I promised him that I wouldn't call him back this time." He ended with, "And now, my friends, in a phrase I once addressed to others, it's time for me to go."

There was near universal praise for Gore's concession speech. Even conservative columnist Mona Charen almost praised him. After granting it would not undo the damage Gore had done, she said his concession was "the finest speech of his life, prompting thoughts of Shakespeare's words, long associated with the beheaded king of England, Charles I: 'Nothing in his life became him like the leaving it.' As much can be said of Gore's campaign." Presumably she meant nothing in Gore's campaign became him like the leaving of it. But if he was such a villain, as Charen seemed to believe, how could anything gracious become him? Whatever she meant, she seemed confused about the quote she used, since Shakespeare died thirty-three years before Charles I was beheaded in 1649. The quote was Malcolm's in the play *Macbeth* to Malcolm's father, King Duncan of Scotland. The reference was to the late Thane of Cawdor, who was made "late" on Duncan's orders, so that Macbeth could become Thane. Macbeth showed his appreciation by murdering Duncan that very night.

With Florida's 25 electoral votes, Bush had a total of 271 to Gore's 267. The popular vote was Gore 50,996,039 and Bush 50,456,141. Bush thus won the Electoral College majority and lost the popular vote, only the fourth president to do so. The others were Benjamin Harrison, to Grover Cleveland in 1888; Rutherford B. Hayes, to Samuel J. Tilden in 1876; and John Quincy Adams, to Andrew Jackson in 1824. We should note that Tilden's election was stolen, which accounts for its presence in the group, and John Quincy Adams was elected by the House of Representatives, as prescribed by the Constitution, after no person got an Electoral College majority.

Karen Hughes was asked about Gore's beating Bush in the popular vote, and she countered that Bush got more popular votes than Clinton. Yes, Jake Tapper noted, "but not more than Gore."

Bush was the first president with an MBA degree, and he was the second president who was the son of a president. The first was, of course, John Quincy Adams. Finally, the Election from Hell was in most respects the closest one in history, and the only one in which a candidate "unconceded."

Some said the election was further proof that Joseph Stalin, who certainly knew how to keep elections under control, was right when he said, "Those who cast the votes decide nothing. Those who count the votes decide everything."

To end on a lighter note, Bill Clinton said, "The one good thing about the 2000 election was that it gave the Supreme Court the chance to stand up for minority rights."

Summing Up

After eighteen chapters of poking fun at our presidents, it is time to put the record in perspective and end our narrative on a positive note. We have had forty-three administrations by forty-two presidents (Grover Cleveland had two nonconsecutive terms, the only president to do so), and for the most part, Chester Congdon's notion of having a man for the job the dogs won't urinate on has been upheld.

Will Rogers, the great American humorist and homespun philosopher, was fond of saying, "I never met a man I didn't like," which provided an opening for many wits to say of an enemy, "Will Rogers never met him." Will also had the saying, "I only joke about people I like," and that seems to us to be a good plank to run on.

Will Rogers wasn't the only notable figure to have respect for politics and politicians. As mentioned in chapter 1, John Calvin held the field in high esteem. The great sixteenth-century religious leader lectured and wrote on politics and social problems and reportedly said, "The highest profession God calls one to is politics." Even H. L. Mencken, a crusty curmudgeon if there ever was one, had this to say: "There is something about a national convention that is as fascinating as a revival or a hanging. It is vulgar, ugly, stupid, and tedious, to be sure, and yet

CAMPAIGN SLOGANS

(Randy Bish. Reprinted by permission of Newspaper Enterprise Association, Inc.)

suddenly comes a show so gaudy and hilarious, so melodramatic and obscene, so unimaginably exhilarating and preposterous, that one lives a gorgeous year in an hour."

Thomas Jefferson had been president but a few months in 1801, when the Reverend Timothy Dwight, then president of Yale, announced that, "We have now reached the consummation of democratic blessedness. We have a country governed by blockheads and knaves; the ties of marriage with all its felicities are severed and destroyed; our wives and daughters are thrown into the stews; our children cast into the world from the breast and forgotten; filial piety is extinguished, and our surnames, the only mark of distinction among families, are abolished. Can the imagination paint anything more dreadful on this side of hell?" It is difficult to believe that it could.

Jefferson was not only a great president but he was one of our greatest men. He wrote the Declaration of Independence, presided over the Louisiana Purchase, which doubled the size of our country, and

"I'm sick of the same old choices...I'm voting for Ross Perot!"

Cynicism, 1992 style (© *The Record*, Jimmy Margulies).

was one of the greatest intellectuals in the country's history. The Reverend Dwight, except for a few hymns he wrote, is long ago forgotten by most Americans.

Our political woes of today cannot begin to match those of 1861, when states were seceding from the Union and a great war threatened to destroy our country. Again we were fortunate in our choice of leaders. After a string of mediocre presidents, from Van Buren to Buchanan, with the single bright exception of James K. Polk, Abraham Lincoln emerged, with the courage and determination to save the nation. "In your hands, my dissatisfied fellow countrymen, and not in mine, is the momentous issue of civil war," he said in his inaugural address. "You have no oath registered in heaven to destroy the government, while I shall have the most solemn one to 'preserve, protect, and defend' it."

Historians have for decades rated Lincoln, mercilessly attacked in his day as "a country clown" and "a baboon," as our greatest president. Also, if he isn't our greatest writer, he certainly ranks with the best.

In spite of the huge debt legacy of the 1980s, our economic troubles certainly have not reached the desperate depths of the Great Depression of the 1930s, when 25 percent of the working force was unemployed. At that point Franklin D. Roosevelt arrived on the scene and assured us that, "This great Nation will endure as it has endured, will revive and will prosper. So first of all, let me assert my firm belief that the only thing we have to fear is fear itself." Roosevelt was also at the helm on December 7, 1941, when the message was received that shook the United States as nothing had since the firing on Fort Sumter that started the Civil War: "Air Raid, Pearl Harbor—This Is No Drill." We thus became the principal power in the greatest war the world has ever seen. And again, Roosevelt reassured us: "Hostilities exist. There is no blinking at the fact that our people, our territory, and our interests are in grave danger. With confidence in our armed forces—with the unbounding determination of our people—we will gain the inevitable triumph—so help us God."

One of the bleakest periods in our history must have occurred in the early stages of the American Revolution, when in December 1776 General George Washington abandoned New York to the British and began his retreat across New Jersey with his ragtag army. Most American colonists probably thought their revolution was over when it had hardly begun. Thomas Paine, who was in Washington's army, wrote, "These are the times that try men's souls. The summer soldier and the sunshine patriot will, in this crisis, shrink from the service of his country; but he that stands by it now, deserves the love and thanks of man and woman. Tyranny, like hell, is not easily conquered; yet we have this consolation with us, that the harder the conflict the more glorious the triumph."

Statements (Paul Conrad. Copyright 1998, Tribune Media Services. Reprinted with permission.)

Johann Rall, the commander of the Hessians at Trenton, scoffed at reports that Washington's army was nearby, noting that he had nothing to fear from "these country clowns." But on Christmas night, in a violent storm, those "country clowns" crossed the Delaware River and the next morning captured or killed the entire Hessian regiment without the loss of a single American life. A brief review of the battle was issued by one of the Americans: "Hessian population of Trenton at 8 A.M., 1,408 men and 39 officers; Hessian population at 9 A.M.—zero."

This was the same George Washington who later was depicted sitting in a wheelbarrow being pushed by his friend David Humphreys. The cartoon, now lost to history, carried the caption, "The glorious time has come to pass when David shall conduct an ass." Suffice it to say that George Washington is the greatest American in history.

To be sure, we have had some ordinary presidents, some below-average presidents, and a few presidents who were failures. But our system has also produced a disproportionately large number of great and near-great presidents, like Lincoln, Washington, Franklin Roosevelt, Jefferson, Jackson, Truman, Polk, Wilson, and Theodore Roosevelt. Most of our presidents have grown in office and been equal to the tasks demanded of them. They were there when we needed them. Perhaps

Benjamin Harrison was correct in his 1888 observation that "Providence has provided" for us. Thus the ancient quote used by John Kennedy in his last official words—his undelivered speech in Dallas—may be most appropriate: "Unless the Lord keep the city, the watchman waketh but in vain."

We'll have great presidents again, as Jackie Kennedy observed in 1963, which is a good note on which to end. The Lord has kept our city, and "this great Nation will endure as it has endured, will revive and will prosper."

Epilogue: Presidential Gallery

As a final note on our presidents, we give in this section a picture of each of the forty-two men, from George Washington to George W. Bush, who have occupied our highest office. We also include for each president a short comment about him made by one of his contemporaries. We have listed the presidents in the order of their ranking in a 1991 poll of the country's leading historians, conducted by Professor Tim H. Blessing, director, Presidential Performance Study, Penn State Berks Campus, Reading, Pennsylvania. In the poll the presidents are also classified as great, near great, above average, average, below average, and failure. William Henry Harrison and James A. Garfield are unranked because of their brief tenure in office, and the Bushes and Clinton are not ranked because of the timing of the poll. There are later polls but those readily available do not classify the presidents according to their degrees of greatness. Also, the later polls do not deviate much from this one.

The photographs of Eisenhower, Kennedy, Lyndon Johnson, Nixon, Ford, Carter, and Reagan, are from the *Pocket Congressional Directory*; those of the Bushes and Clinton are from the *Public Papers of the Presidents*; those of Washington, John Adams, Jefferson, Madison, and

Monroe are copies of Gilbert Stuart paintings; and that of John Quincy Adams is a copy of a painting by Thomas Sully. The pictures of Taylor and Andrew Johnson are from engravings by Alexander H. Ritchie, and that of Buchanan is from an engraving by John C. Buttre. Jackson's, Van Buren's, and Polk's pictures are copies of daguerreotypes by Mathew Brady, and Lincoln's is a copy of a photograph by Alexander Gardner. The originals of Arthur and Wilson belong to the New York Historical Society, that of Franklin Roosevelt is in the Franklin D. Roosevelt Library, and the remaining photographs are in the Library of Congress.

The ranking is as follows:

GREAT
1. Lincoln
2. F. Roosevelt
3. Washington
4. Jefferson

NEAR GREAT
5. T. Roosevelt
6. Wilson
7. Jackson
8. Truman

ABOVE AVERAGE
9. J. Adams
10. L. Johnson
11. Eisenhower
12. Polk
13. Kennedy
14. Madison
15. Monroe
16. J. Q. Adams
17. Cleveland

AVERAGE
18. McKinley
19. Taft
20. Van Buren
21. Hoover
22. Hayes
23. Arthur
24. Ford
25. Carter
26. B. Harrison

BELOW AVERAGE
27. Taylor
28. Reagan
29. Tyler
30. Fillmore
31. Coolidge
32. Pierce

FAILURE
33. A. Johnson
34. Buchanan
35. Nixon
36. Grant
37. Harding

UNRANKED
38. William Henry Harrison
39. James A. Garfield
40. George H. W. Bush
41. Bill Clinton
42. George W. Bush

Abraham Lincoln 1861–1865
"A low-bred obscene clown."
(Atlanta Intelligencer)

Franklin D. Roosevelt 1933–1945
He thinks the government is "a milk
cow with 125 million teats."
(H. L. Mencken)

George Washington 1789–1797
"The man who is the source of all
the misfortunes of our country."
(Philadelphia Aurora)

Thomas Jefferson 1801–1809
"A contemptible hypocrite," with
"pretensions to character."
(Alexander Hamilton)

Theodore Roosevelt 1901–1909
"As sweet a gentleman as ever
scuttled a ship or cut a throat."
(Henry Watterson)

Woodrow Wilson 1913–1921
"He talked like Jesus Christ,
but acted like Lloyd George."
(French Premier Georges Clemenceau)

Andrew Jackson 1829–1837
"A barbarian and savage who can
scarcely spell his own name."
(John Quincy Adams)

Harry S. Truman 1945–1953
"The poorest president since
George Washington."
(Congressman Charlie Halleck)

John Adams 1797–1801
"One of the most egregious
fools upon the continent."
(James Thomson Callender)

Lyndon B. Johnson 1963–1969
He "had so much power and wanted so
much more power that Democrats did-
n't know whether to vote for him or
plug him in." (Barry Goldwater)

Dwight D. Eisenhower
1953–1961
"He couldn't make a decision to save
his soul in hell." (Harry S. Truman)

James K. Polk 1845–1849
"A victim of the use of water as
a beverage." (Sam Houston)

John F. Kennedy 1961–1963
He impersonates "a prematurely elder
statesman who wants to grow up
to be Lyndon Johnson."
(New York Post)

James Madison 1809–1817
"A withered little applejohn."
(Washington Irving)

James Monroe 1817–1825
"A damned infernal old scoundrel."
(Secretary of the Treasury
William H. Crawford)

John Quincy Adams 1825–1829
"The Pimp of the Coalition."
(Andrew Jackson supporters)

Grover Cleveland 1885–1889, 1893–1897
"A coarse debauchee who would bring his harlots with him to Washington and hire lodgings for them convenient to the White House." *(New York Sun)*

William McKinley 1897–1901
"A white-livered cur with no more backbone than a chocolate éclair."
(Theodore Roosevelt)

William Howard Taft 1909–1913
"Fat son of a bitch, ain't he?"
(Clarence Darrow)

Martin Van Buren 1837–1841
"A fop laced up in corsets, such as women in town wear, and if possible, tighter than the best of them."
(Davy Crockett)

Herbert Hoover 1929–1933
"In Hoover we trusted. Now we are
busted." (1932 placard)

Rutherford B. Hayes 1877–1881
"Rutherfraud."
(Tilden supporters)

Chester A. Arthur 1881–1885
"A nonentity with side whiskers."
(Woodrow Wilson)

Gerald R. Ford 1974–1977
"The man who pardoned Nixon."
(Ronald Reagan)

Jimmy Carter 1977–1981
He "couldn't get the Pledge of
Allegiance through Congress."
(A veteran congressman)

Benjamin Harrison 1889–1893
"A purely intellectual being with no
bowels," whose reelection would mean
"four more years in a dripping cave."
(An 1892 contemporary)

Zachary Taylor 1849–1850
"Dead and in hell, and I am glad of it."
(Brigham Young)

Ronald Reagan 1981–1989
"An amiable dunce." (Ex-Secretary
of Defense Clark Clifford)

John Tyler 1841–1845
"His Accidency."
(John Quincy Adams)

Millard Fillmore 1850–1853
"A vain and handsome mediocrity."
(Thurlow Weed)

Calvin Coolidge 1923–1929
"The greatest man ever to come
out of Plymouth Notch, Vermont."
(Clarence Darrow)

Franklin Pierce 1853–1857
If he can be nominated, "no private
citizen is safe" from the office.
(Stephen A. Douglas)

Andrew Johnson 1865–1869
"Dirty as cart-wheel grease."
(A radical Republican)

James Buchanan 1857–1861
"An able man, but is in small matters
without judgment and sometimes acts
like an old maid." (James K. Polk)

Richard M. Nixon 1969–1974
He "should get his ass out of the
White House—today!"
(Barry Goldwater)

Ulysses S. Grant 1869–1877
His election gives us a chance to "see if
there is any difference between a drunken
tailor [Andrew Johnson] and a drunken
tanner." (General Benjamin Butler)

Warren G. Harding 1921–1923
"Not a bad man. He was just a slob."
(Alice Roosevelt Longworth)

William Henry Harrison 1841
Regret his death "only because he did
not live long enough to prove his incapacity for the office of President."
(William Cullen Bryant)

James A. Garfield 1881
"Not possessed of the backbone of an
angle-worm." (U. S. Grant)

George H. W. Bush 1989–1993
"He reminds every woman of her first
husband." (Humorist Art Buchwald)

Bill Clinton 1993–2001
"He'll turn the White House into the
Waffle House." (George H. W. Bush)

George W. Bush 2001–
"The worst president in all of American
history." (Helen Thomas, dean of
the White House Press Corps)

Bibliography

Abels, Jules. *Out of the Jaws of Victory*. New York: Henry Holt, 1959.

————. *The Degeneration of Our Presidential Election: A History and Analysis of an American Institution in Trouble*. New York: Macmillan, 1968.

Acheson, Dean. *A Democrat Looks at His Party*. New York: Harper & Brothers, 1955.

————. *Present at the Creation*. New York: W.W. Norton, 1969.

Adler, Bill. *The Kennedy Wit*. New York: Citadel Press, 1964.

Agar, Herbert. *The People's Choice, from Washington to Harding*. New York: Houghton Mifflin, 1933.

Anderson, Donald F. *William Howard Taft*. Ithaca, N.Y.: Cornell University Press, 1973.

Armbruster, Maxim Ethan. *The Presidents of the United States and Their Administrations from Washington to Reagan*. New York: Horizon Press, 1982.

Bailey, Thomas A. *Presidential Greatness: The Image and the Man from George Washington to the Present*. New York: Appleton-Century, 1966.

Baker, Peter. *The Breach: Inside the Impeachment and Trial of William Jefferson Clinton*. New York: Scribner, 2000.

Bassett, Margaret Byrd. *Profiles and Portraits of American Presidents*. New York: McKay, 1976.

Bendiner, Robert. *White House Fever*. New York: Harcourt, Brace, 1960.

Ben-Veniste, Richard, and George Frampton Jr. *Stonewall: The Real Story of the Watergate Prosecution.* New York: Simon and Schuster, 1977.

Boller, Paul F., Jr. *Presidential Anecdotes.* New York: Oxford University Press, 1981.

Bugliosi, Vincent. *No Island of Sanity.* New York: Ballantine Publishing Group, 1998.

———. *The Betrayal of America: How the Supreme Court Undermined the Constitution and Chose Our President.* New York: Thunder's Mouth Press, 2001.

Burns, James MacGregor. *Roosevelt: The Lion and the Fox.* New York: Harcourt, Brace, 1956.

Butterfield, Roger P. *The American Past: A History of the United States from Concord to Hiroshima, 1775-1945.* New York: Simon and Schuster, 1947.

Cirker, Hayward, and Blanche Cirker. *Dictionary of American Portraits.* New York: Dover Publications, 1967.

Cohn, David L. *The Fabulous Democrats.* New York: G.P. Putnam's Sons, 1956.

Cunliffe, Marcus. *American Presidents and the Presidency,* 2nd ed. New York: McGraw-Hill, 1976.

DiSalle, Michael V., with Lawrence G. Blochman. *Second Choice.* New York: Hawthorne Books, 1966.

Dole, Robert. *Great Political Wit: Laughing (Almost) All the Way to the White House.* Rockland, Mass.: Compass Press, 1999.

Dorman, Michael. *The Second Man: The Changing Role of the Vice Presidency.* New York: Delacorte, 1968.

Duffy, Herbert S. *William Howard Taft.* New York: Minton, Balch, 1930.

Durant, John, and Alice Durant. *Pictorial History of American Presidents.* New York: A.S. Barnes, 1955.

Eaton, Herbert. *Presidential Timber: A History of Nominating Conventions, 1868-1960.* New York: Free Press of Glencoe, 1964.

Ehrenreich, Barbara. *The Worst Years of Our Lives: Irreverent Notes from a Decade of Greed.* New York: Pantheon Books, 1990.

Ernst, Morris Leopold. *The People Know Best: The Ballots vs. the Polls.* Washington, D.C.: Public Affairs Press, 1949.

Felknor, Bruce L. *Dirty Politics.* New York: W.W. Norton, 1966.

———. *Smear, Sabotage, and Reform in U.S. Elections.* New York: Praeger, 1992.

Gable, John A. *The Bull Moose Years: Theodore Roosevelt and the Progressive Party.* Port Washington, N.Y.: Kennikat Press, 1978.

Germond, Jack W., and Jules Witcover. *Whose Broad Stripes and Bright Stars? The Trivial Pursuit of the Presidency, 1988.* New York: Warner Books, 1989.

———. *Mad as Hell: Revolt at the Ballot Box, 1992.* New York: Warner Books, Inc., 1993.

Gibson, Albert M. *A Political Crime: The History of the Great Fraud.* New York: W.S. Gottsberger, 1885.

Goodman, Mark, ed. *Give 'Em Hell, Harry!* New York: Award Books, 1975.

Gunderson, Robert G. *The Log-Cabin Campaign.* Lexington: University of Kentucky Press, 1957.

Harris, Leon A., Jr. *The Fine Art of Political Wit.* New York: Bell Publishing Co., 1964.

Harwood, Richard, ed. *The Pursuit of the Presidency 1980.* New York: Berkley Books, 1980.

Haworth, Paul L. *The Hayes-Tilden Election.* Indianapolis: Bobbs-Merrill, 1927.

Holland, Barbara. *Hail to the Chiefs: How to Tell Your Polks from Your Tylers.* New York: Ballantine Books, 1990.

Hoyt, Edwin P. *Jumbos and Jackasses.* Garden City, N.Y.: Doubleday, 1960.

Jeffers, H. Paul. *An Honest President: The Life and Presidencies of Grover Cleveland.* New York: William Morrow, 2000.

Johnson, Gerald W. *Roosevelt: Dictator or Democrat.* New York: Harper & Brothers, 1941.

Johnson, Haynes. *The Best of Times: America in the Clinton Years.* New York: Harcourt, 2001.

Josephson, Matthew. *The Politicos, 1865–1896.* New York: Harcourt, Brace, 1938.

Judah, Charles Burnet, and George W. Smith. *The Unchosen.* New York: Coward-McCann, 1962.

Kane, Joseph Nathan. *Facts About the Presidents: A Compilation of Biographical and Historical Data.* New York: H.W. Wilson, 1981.

Kaul, Donald W. *They're All in It Together: When Good Things Happen to Bad People.* Kansas City: Andrews and McMeel, 1991.

Kelly, Frank K. *The Fight for the White House: The Story of 1912.* New York: Crowell, 1961.

Lacey, Robert and Danny Danziger. *The Year 1000: What Life was Like at the Turn of the First Millennium.* Boston: Little, Brown, 1999.

Leish, Kenneth W., ed. *The American Heritage Pictorial History of the Presidents of the United States.* New York: American Heritage Publishing Co., 1968.

Lewis, Charles. *The Buying of the President 2000.* New York: Avon Books, 2000.

Lewis, Michael. *Trail Fever.* New York: Alfred A. Knopf, 1997.

Lorant, Stefan. *The Glorious Burden: The American Presidency.* New York: Harper and Row, 1968.

Lowe, Jacques. *Portrait: The Emergence of John F. Kennedy.* New York: Bramhall House, 1961.

Lurie, Leonard. *The Running of Richard Nixon.* New York: Coward, McCann and Geoghegan, 1972.

Mankiewicz, Frank. *Perfectly Clear: Nixon from Whittier to Watergate.* New York: Quadrangle, New York Times Book Co., 1973.

McCombs, William F. *Making Woodrow Wilson President.* New York: Fairview, 1921.

McCormac, Eugene I. *James K. Polk: A Political Biography.* Berkeley: University of California Press, 1922.

McCoy, Charles A. *Polk and the Presidency.* Austin: University of Texas Press, 1960.

McCoy, Donald R. *Calvin Coolidge: The Quiet President.* New York: Macmillan, 1967.

McCullough, David. *Truman.* New York: Simon and Schuster, 1992.

———. *John Adams.* New York: Simon and Schuster, 2001.

McGinniss, Joe. *The Selling of the President 1968.* New York: Trident Press, 1969.

Melder, Keith. *Hail to the Candidate: Presidential Campaigns from Banners to Broadcasts.* Washington, D.C.: Smithsonian Institution Press, 1992.

Mencken, H. L. *A Carnival of Buncombe,* ed. Malcolm Moos. Baltimore: Johns Hopkins Press, 1956.

Merzer, Martin, ed. *The Miami Herald Report: Democracy Held Hostage.* New York: St. Martin's Press, 2001.

Miller, Hope Ridings. *Scandals in the Highest Office: Facts and Fictions in the Private Lives of Our Presidents.* New York: Random House, 1973.

Miller, Mark Crispin. *The Bush Dyslexicon: Observations on a National Disorder.* New York: W.W. Norton, 2002.

Miller, Merle. *Plain Speaking: An Oral Biography of Harry S. Truman.* New York: Berkley Publishing Corp., 1973.

Mollenhoff, Clark R. *The Man Who Pardoned Nixon.* New York: St. Martin's Press, 1976.

Moore, Edmund A. *A Catholic Runs for President.* New York: Ronald Press, 1956.

Moore, Jonathan, and Janet Fraser, eds. *Campaign for President.* Cambridge, Mass.: Ballinger Publishing Co., 1977.

Moos, Malcolm. *The Republicans: A History of Their Party.* New York: Random House, 1956.

Morgan, James. *Our Presidents.* New York: Macmillan Co., 1969.

Morison, Samuel Eliot. *The Oxford History of the American People.* New York: Oxford University Press, 1965.

Morrel, Martha McBride. *"Young Hickory." The Life and Times of President James K. Polk.* New York: E.P. Dutton, 1949.

Moscow, Warren. *Roosevelt and Willkie.* Englewood Cliffs, N.J.: Prentice-Hall, Inc., 1968.

Murray, Robert K. *The Harding Era: Warren G. Harding and His Administration.*
Minneapolis: University of Minnesota Press, 1969.

Myers, William S. *The Republican Party.* New York: Century Co., 1931.

Nichols, John. *Jews for Buchanan.* New York: New Press, 2001.

O'Donnell, Kenneth P., and David F. Powers. *Johnny, We Hardly Knew Ye.* New
York: Pocket Book, 1973.

Olive, David. *Political Babble: The 1,000 Dumbest Things Ever Said by Politicians.*
John Wiley & Sons, Inc., 1992.

Parmet, Herbert S. *Never Again: A President Runs for a Third Term.* New York:
Macmillan, 1968.

Paysinger, Mildred A. *You May Quote Me—the Politicians.* Hicksville, N.Y.:
Exposition Press, 1974.

Redding, Jack. *Inside the Democratic Party.* Indianapolis: Bobbs-Merrill, 1958.

Remini, Robert V. *The Election of Andrew Jackson.* Philadelphia: Lippincott,
1963.

Rienow, Robert, and Leona Train Rienow. *The Lonely Quest: The Evolution of
Presidential Leadership.* Chicago: Follett Publishing Co., 1966.

Rogers, Will. *How We Elect Our Presidents.* Boston: Little, Brown, 1952.

Roseboom, Eugene H. *A History of Presidential Elections.* New York: Macmillan,
1957.

Ross, Irwin. *The Loneliest Campaign: The Truman Victory of 1948.* New York:
New American Library, 1968.

Sabato, Larry J., ed. *Overtime! The Election 2000 Thriller.* New York: Longman
Publishers, 2002.

Sandberg, Carl. *Abraham Lincoln: The War Years,* 4 vols. New York: Harcourt,
Brace, 1939.

Scheer, Robert. "Jimmy Carter: A Candid Conversation with the Democratic
Candidate for President." *Playboy,* November 1976, 63–86.

Schlesinger, Arthur M., Jr. *A Thousand Days.* Boston: Houghton Mifflin, 1965.

Sellers, Charles. *James K. Polk, Continentalist, 1843–1846.* Princeton, N.J.:
Princeton University Press, 1957.

Shogan, Robert. *Bad News: Where the Press Goes Wrong in the Making of the
President.* Chicago: Ivan R. Dee, 2001.

Sinclair, Andrew. *The Available Man: The Life Behind the Mask of Warren
Gamaliel Harding.* New York: Macmillan, 1965.

Sirica, John J. *To Set the Record Straight.* New York: W.W. Norton, 1979.

Smith, Page. *A New Age Now Begins,* 2 vols. New York: McGraw-Hill, 1976.

Sorenson, Theodore C. *Kennedy.* New York: Harper and Row, 1965.

Stone, Irving. *Clarence Darrow for the Defense.* Garden City, N.Y.: Doubleday, 1941.

————. *They Also Ran*. New York: Pyramid Books, 1964.

Summers, Anthony, with Robbyn Swan. *The Arrogance of Power: The Secret World of Richard Nixon*. New York: Penguin Books, 2000.

Tapper, Jake. *Down and Dirty: The Plot to Steal the Presidency*. Boston: Little, Brown, 2001.

Taylor, John M. *Garfield of Ohio, the Available Man*. New York: W.W. Norton, 1970.

Toobin, Jeffrey. *Too Close to Call: The Thirty-Six-Day Battle to Decide the 2000 Election*. New York: Random House, 2001.

Trager, James. *The People's Chronology: A Year-by-Year Record of Human Events from Prehistory to the Present*. New York: Holt, Rinehart and Winston, 1979.

Truman, Margaret. *Harry S. Truman*. New York: William Morrow, 1973.

Tugwell, Rexford Guy. *How They Became President: Thirty-Five Ways to the White House*. New York: Simon and Schuster, 1968.

Udall, Morris K., with Bob Neuman and Randy Udall. *Too Funny to Be President*. New York: Henry Holt, 1988.

Van Deusen, Glyndon G. *Thurlow Weed: Wizard of the Lobby*. Boston: Little, Brown, 1947.

Warren, Sidney. *The Battle for the Presidency*. Philadelphia: J. B. Lippincott, 1968.

Weisbord, Marvin R. *Campaigning for President: A New Look at the Road to the White House*. Washington, D.C.: Public Affairs Press, 1964.

White, Theodore H. *Breach of Faith: The Fall of Richard Nixon*. New York: Atheneum Publishers, 1975.

————. *The Making of the President 1960*. New York: Atheneum Publishers, 1961.

————. *The Making of the President 1964*. New York: Atheneum Publishers, 1965.

————. *The Making of the President 1968*. New York: Atheneum Publishers, 1969.

————. *The Making of the President 1972*. New York: Atheneum Publishers, 1973.

Whitney, David C. *The American Presidents*. Garden City, N.Y.: Doubleday, 1975.

Witcover, Jules. *Marathon: The Pursuit of the Presidency 1972–1976*. New York: Viking Press, 1977.

Zornow, William F. *Lincoln and the Party Divided*. Norman: University of Oklahoma Press, 1954.

Index

Page numbers in italic indicate an illustration.

239

About the Authors

DAVID E. JOHNSON and JOHNNY R. JOHNSON are retired college professors living in Birmingham and Florence, Alabama, respectively. In addition to writing presidential history, they have published many technical books in the fields of mathematics and engineering.